FREEING OUR
FROZEN SONGS

FREEING OUR FROZEN SONGS

TRANSMUTING PAIN TO POWER

An Anthology of Poetry and Visual Art

Co-Created By

Meg Bishop

Kirsten Fountain

Crystal Gasser

McKenzie Lee

Kaya Miranda

Mikell Nielsen

JC Smith

Abigail Spencer

Kaiden Valenzuela

Terah Van Dusen

Curated by Kirsten Fountain

WRIGHTWOOD PRESS

ANN ARBOR

Headshot photography credits are as follows: Mikell Nielsen (pages 1 and 185); Kirsten Fountain (pages 23, 105, 145, 165); Kaya Miranda (page 43); Emily Prosise (page 63); Abigail Spencer (page 83); Meg Bishop (page 125).

Final interior design and typesetting by Kirsten Fountain, with support from Mikell Nielsen.

Curator's note: This publication is not intended as a substitute for advice from healthcare professionals.

November 2025
ISBN 978-1-962996-13-6 (Softcover)
ISBN 978-1-962996-12-9 (Hardcover)
ISBN 978-1-962996-14-3 (eBook)

Publication Acknowledgements

Our co-creators made this project possible. Because of all of you, I will never be the same. I am forever grateful for the time and energy you dedicated to this work, for your belief in me and yourselves, and for your willingness to follow me into the darkness to find our light.

My child, Kaiden, courageously entered into this space of intentional confrontation of myself, my parenting, and the impacts it had on both of us, and came out with me on the other side with more wisdom, love, empathy, and acceptance for each other than I ever knew possible. Tim, my husband, is my greatest cheerleader, space-holder, talk-processing partner, and defender. He has witnessed my darkness and is warmed by my light. Ruth and Sara, my mother and sister, relived it all with me, then supported me as I created and shared, which was incredibly challenging, rewarding, and healing.

Erin Zelinka is my brave, deep-diving, writing, and healing partner. Thank you for your wisdom, expertise, and insight with the written word, and for meeting me in my darkness and leading me to my light.

Barbara Holiday donated her time to edit our manuscript and guide me through the writing, formatting, and publishing world as the beginner I was at the outset of this project. Your support has been invaluable.

Mikell Nielsen got into the weeds of formatting and book cover design with me. Bearing and sharing the load is twice as fun when I can do it with you.

JC Smith managed to support our poetry critique circles and edit our poetry alongside me while also living a full life with her children and a very demanding full-time job. I could not be more grateful for your wisdom, support, and friendship.

McKenzie Lee helped me create the Kickstarter and lent her ethereal music to our book trailer, all while creating her own music videos (and a tiny human), and then continued her support with a newborn in her arms. Your friendship and expertise have been a lifeline for me during this project.

Our beta readers, Mateo Luke, Nicole Rensenbrink, Erin Zelinka, Celeste Ryane, Monica Haley, Amanda Pitt, and Jill Wilde, your wisdom, insight, willingness to share your input even when it was uncomfortable, as well as the time, energy, and dedication you gave to our project, will always be an epically profound gift. I am utterly grateful and in awe of you all!

Jill Wilde, your incredible generosity has left an indelible mark on my heart and soul. Thank you for all that you are and do.

Maurice York, my precious Cousin, thank you for publishing our anthology. Your support is priceless.

And to all of our Kickstarter backers, thank you for believing in us enough to invest in our art and success.

A Winter Blessing

By Kirsten Fountain

When winter's as deep
As the night is long
And cold threatens
To freeze your song

May memories of spring delight your soul
Verdant hills with butterflies aflutter
Bulbs bursting into brilliant blooms
Bees buzzing and bathing in nectar

May the summer sun's
Warm and golden rays
Caress you gently
On your darkest days

May fall's kiss linger
A soft reminder
Colorful and crisp falling leaves
Symbolize needed surrender

May the sweetness of life meet you
In the bitterness of winter-long
Slowly warming your heart
Freeing your frozen song

"When we begin listening to each other, and when we talk about the things that matter to us, the world begins to change."

Margaret Wheatley, Ed.D.

TABLE OF CONTENTS

INTRODUCTION

By Kirsten Fountain

This book contains our stories
Stories of survival
Stories that forged us
Stories that formed us
Stories that free us

Our voices
Our pain
Our pasts
Our shame

Once frozen in fear
Finally free to fly

What do you do when your body can no longer house the brutalities of the life you have lived? This book is for readers who have experienced the darkness of trauma. It is also for those who want to better understand the impact of trauma on survivors. Our book is intended to support readers who are on the path toward the end of this darkness where light, healing, and hope can be found. Collectively, our co-creators confronted and freed what had long been frozen inside us. Our stories are now held within this book, and our bodies are lighter.

The pandemic allowed me the space to embrace a new healing season within my soul. With conviction, I began to confront the healing needs I had put off for another time. I awoke on the winter solstice of 2020, wondering what to do with the cold, lonely two weeks of winter break ahead of me. As an educator, these weeks had always offered me a time of respite and renewal. While still lounging in bed, I lazily scrolled through social media. A post caught my eye about harnessing the power of the winter solstice to call in the best of the seasons ahead. Inspired, I decided to take the advice in the caption of that post. I intentionally sat in front of my computer and invited creativity to speak to me as I moved my fingers. Within a few hours, I developed a presentation that included the theme and concepts of this anthology to share with the beautiful beings I wanted to join me in this project. This work represents my decision to continue my healing journey in community. I hoped to work with my child, my chosen children, a former colleague, and some of my former students and their family members. I was amazed and inspired as each treasured person I asked to participate responded with a resounding, "YES!"

Not one of the ten of us had any idea what we were getting ourselves into.

We have experienced profound pain. We are not afraid of confronting this pain; rather, we are terrified of what might happen if we don't. Some of us are poets, some are visual artists, and some combined both gifts as we dug for and then dragged our wounds into the light to be seen, felt, and released. Each chapter of our book represents an individual's study of light and dark. That which forms us and is formed by us. That which has been, is, and will be. That which was once frozen and is now free.

We decided to meet once a month to confront our pain and transmute it into our power with support and solidarity. Seeking and finding our root wounds deep within the soil of our pasts, we identified how they continue to grow in our present so we could intentionally create new possibilities for our future. Therefore, each of our stories is a complete chapter organized into the following sections: Past, Present, and Possible. For us, the magic came in that final section, where the powers of transmutation and manifestation combined to support the creation of new possibilities.

As a mother, my journey through creating this book has been brutal and beautiful. Not only have I been able to confront and begin to transmute the root wounds of my childhood, but I have been able to come alongside my child, Kaiden, as they did the same. As we evolve, language naturally evolves with us. My child's pronouns have evolved as they have evolved. The following is my attempt to describe the profound importance of this evolutionary process through the medium my heart knows best.

Constructs Constrict

My child is free to Be
The pronouns they/them/their
Capture just one aspect of their identity
A current construct they choose to wear

We exist in a plane
Of human construction
We wax and we wane
With limited perception and conception

Coloring outside accepted bounds
Only defined by their heart, soul, and mind
So much more than a pronoun
Solid ground they find

Society
Does not define
Their reality

Uninhibited by
Perceptions
Conceptions
Constructs
Created
By humans
Like you and me
My child is free to Be

As a survivor of trauma and as the mother of a survivor of trauma, I learned that there is a deep need for those who hurt us to take accountability for their impact on our lives. That isn't always possible or practical. In my case, I decided to do my best to take accountability for how my own trauma impacted myself and those I Love. Then, I began to show up for myself in the ways I had needed a father to show up for me as a child, which meant confronting worthiness within myself. Was I worthy of receiving my own Love?

I had to confront the guilt and shame of my inability to show up as the mother my child needed when they faced their traumas and then take accountability for its impact on them. I learned from and with my child that my feelings of shame and guilt as a parent do not serve my child, and they certainly do not serve me. Those feelings are authentic and valid. They are teachers. I came to learn that they must be felt, learned from, and then released before they can do further damage to myself and my child.

After I worked through those emotions, I could show up for my child as the woman and mother I am today, holding them in the secure embrace of unconditional Love and security that I could not provide when I was younger. The very same secure embrace in which I continue to hold my little girl self today. Because I AM worthy of receiving my own Love. So are you. We all are.

So, rather than accountability, I have found something far more valuable: acceptance through release. I release the need for someone else to release me. I release the pain and shame that have kept me small. I release the words and feelings that I kept imprisoned in my body's cells for five long decades. I accept closure and forgiveness from myself, for myself. In return, I accept a more peaceful, intentional life that I live for myself and those I love.

We believe that everyone can access this healing. We created this book in order to empower ourselves, each other, and our readers through our creative healing efforts. This anthology is the tangible outcome of our intangible, ongoing healing. We believe this work is just the beginning. The door is now open for this healing to impact our families, future generations, and even those who came before us.

Our intention is that compassion, empathy, accountability, acceptance, and release continue to grow in each of us, moving through whatever comes next as this work makes its way into the world. Our hope for our readers is the same. It is our experience that when we heal individually, it inspires healing collectively.

Spoiler alert
We are not
surviving,
we are
T H R I V I N G.
We are not
victims,
we are
V I C T O R I O U S.
(Most of the time)

For more information about this project, visit freeingourfrozensongs.com.

An Invitation for Self-Care

While experiencing our book, you will read, see, and feel
words and images that are arresting. These pages hold our
truths. We came together to intentionally transmute our brutal
realities into beautiful realizations. Therefore, our art may
contain images, including nudity, language, and descriptions
of events, that may be disturbing to some readers.

Please take care of yourself while you read.

BEING

Journaling As You Read

Before we begin, we invite you to be a human being, being human with us. The words "begin" and "being" are made up of the same letters, which allows us to remember the importance of the beginning in being human. If we adopt a beginner's mindset, we begin anew as often as we desire to recreate, rewrite, and rewire ourselves as we continue this human experience. As you consider your own beginning as a human being, what comes to your mind as the root wounds you would like to dig into as you experience this book with us?

Creativity is empowering and powerful. Intentionally inviting creativity into our healing process allowed radical changes and healing to take place in our lives. If you would like to invite creativity to support you as you read, we encourage you to listen to the urges in your body, heart, mind, and soul that call to you for a creative outlet, then answer that call as you feel led. It is our hope that your own unique form of creativity is sparked as you read.

If journaling calls to you as you process our art, a companion workbook, *Freeing My Frozen Songs: Transmuting Pain to Power*, is available on our website, www.freeingourfrozensongs.com. It contains reflection questions, space to create, and many practices we utilized as we did this work. It also provides insight into our pain-to-power process. Journaling can be a powerful tool, especially when paired with trauma-informed therapy or counseling. If meditation is supportive, we created two meditations with a singing bowl practitioner specifically to support our readers. They are also available on our website.

Together, we open the door to healing ourselves, our families, ancestors, and the generations to come. We invite you to cross this threshold with us as we courageously enter into a whole new world of our intentional creation. Come, rise with us.

MIKELL NIELSEN

BIOGRAPHY

Mikell Nielsen (she/her) was only 5 years old when she watched her grandfather develop film in his darkroom, but the experience left a vivid impression on her. She was absolutely mesmerized by the process: the red light, the smell of chemicals, the paper rocking back and forth, and finally an image that magically appeared. Her grandfather, Horace Overacker, was an engineer by trade and a photographer at heart. Though he passed away in 1974, his images, to this day, embody his creative spirit and help keep not only his memory alive but also the memories of his family and friends whose portraits he took. Inspired by her grandfather, Mikell embraced his passion and became a photographer herself.

At the beginning of her career, Mikell's main focus was portraiture, including families, couples, and weddings. She eventually found herself adding fashion and commercial photography to her repertoire under the name Rebel Louise Photography. She owned and operated two photography studios in southern Oregon, but when the pandemic hit, it changed her course. Mikell now finds herself doing what her grandfather loved—taking photos of family and friends and special personal projects.

Prologue

can i play at the school mom

just me and
a kid and her dad
laughing and playing
squeaky metal merry-go-round
chips of wood in my shoe
i spy on them
longing to be part of
their magic

high above my head
the light buzzes on
announcing arrival of
the DARK

i watch that girl and her dad leave
loneliness THICK like quicksand

i STAYED too long
now i have to walk
through a dark hallway
i stand on the edge
cold light turns to darkness
my shoe kicks a rock
the ricochet echo dies off
into scary silence

with PANIC disguised as courage
my legs take off
heart beating fast
pound pound pound
i emerge into remnants
of the day's last bit of light

leaning against a car HE speaks
your mom is busy and told me to
give you a ride home

i hesitantly stop
confusing rules
don't trust strangers

respect adults
do what you are told

i look to his friend
he does not talk
my pants FEEL warm
then wet

pinhole eyes see
stitching
dash no dash
dash no dash
on the DEEP dark seat
bumpy carpet
short thick loops of
dark midnight blue
i smell leather and grease
s w o o s h
my legs pulled
hard
fast

i have ABANDONED myself
my body is gone
watching IT from above
cloud stuck in one spot
HE is wiggly
i can't see me
i can't hear or feel
any thing or any pain

it's eating my brain
swiss cheese memory
big dark EMPTY holes
bits of razor-sharp details
my body starts to buzz
urgently

walking home i am
more alone than before
homes with families
kids playing with kids

mowed lawns
i hear a mom yell *dinner's ready*
i see what i don't have
i feel a deep ACHE

in the bathtub with mr. bubble
my body screams
MY naughty secret
my pee pee
stings like mad bees
hot as lava
throbbing from buried thorns

shame and guilt grow so big
i cannot cry
i cannot tell
i can NOT

mom I lost something
help me find it
i will lead her just close enough
then SHE will find them
and she will know
i NEED her to know

in a field by my school
i planted my pain
partially hidden
partially buried
but DYING to be rescued
my sour bloody undies
a CHUNK of my self
lay in the grass and
r o t t e d

how
　　　did
　　　　　I
　　　　　　　survive

This is when I am supposed to RUN
But these tiny legs turn to lead
This is when I am supposed to FLEE
But this small body has become numb
This is when I am supposed to SCREAM
But this little mouth is frozen shut
This is when my soul evaporates

Lured and Snared
  I do not understand what is happening
  Everything is different
Trapped and Ashamed
  If I make a sound I will fall into the sky
  Everything is upside down

Y e s t e r d a y
I was living in an age of innocence
Was

T o d a y
I know things
Things I should not know

T o m o r r o w
I am damaged goods
Because of you
And our secrets

Hush-hush little one
I am your savior
I am your friend
I am going to help you
Feel happy again

Hush-hush little one
I know my love hurts
I know you don't like it
I know you will soon
Give in and be quiet

Hush-hush little one
I am your master
I am your pal
I am going to
  D r o w n you in mud
  MAT your hair
  Ssscccrrraapppeee your skin with gravel
Pick you up
Hug you
Say that I love you
Again and again

Felt like I was drowning
Something inside my soul made me. . .
  Get up
  Put my clothes back on
  Wipe the tears off my face
  Brush my matted hair
  Slide my feet into my big girl shoes
But they were too big

Hide it
  It will find me
Keep it shut
  It will grow in size
Open it
  Chaos will ensue

hello?
i am here
in the place in between
i see you but it is foggy
i hear you but your voice is muffled
from the place in between
you cannot see me
you cannot hear me
from the place in between
i am here
hello?

Here I am
Stuck
Stagnant
Waiting

I have climbed mountains
I have fought beasts
I have bled
I have cried
I have grown

Yet

Here I am
Stuck
Stagnant
Waiting

you cannot touch
  where I am broken
you cannot hear
  venomous words spoken
you cannot see
  where he touched me
you cannot smell
  the scent of shame
you cannot taste
  my blood as it oozes from my soul
  invisibly staining my skin

My dress, neatly pressed
My hair, tidy and smooth
My makeup, flawless
Not too little
Not too much
I look perfect

It is like deciding to get up and off the couch
  but suddenly wondering why

It is like devouring boxes of donuts
  then shoving my fingers down my throat

It is like eating healthy and exercising
  then battering and bruising my fat legs
  with a rolling pin

It is like pretending to be happy
  with a screeching wicked voice inside my head

It is like acting as though everything is hunky-dory
  when it is a fucking shit show

Two choices
I can stay
or
I can go
but
Tell me
How do I abandon
Part of myself
to
Find myself

Where I was once
  Stuck
  Frozen
  Cemented
I am now Ruler of My Destiny
  Sowing seeds
  Growing strong
  Celebrating
As crowns of flowers
  Bloom at my feet

1966
I was born a nice baby
And then I became a
dumping ground for
the decayed morality of. . .
strangers
friend's brother
babysitter's oldest son
family friend
teenage girl
boys who used me
Chipping away at my soul
Self-worth fading
Becoming smaller and smaller
until i was almost gone

2022
I choose Me
I rebuild Myself
I embrace a Future
without you
E V I C T E D
Your lease is up
Your time has expired
I am no longer yours
I choose Me
Today

I am a beautiful heartbeat

Vital
Electric
Booming
Unyielding
Nourishing
Protecting
Pulsating
Thriving
Fierce

I am a beautiful heartbeat

See Me
I battled my way here
Now I am twice my size
I am a mighty wind
I am everything I need

Rewrite your story.

*Pry the pen from the decaying fist of
the past.*

Who am I to smile?
Who am I to let the gentle
breeze pick up my hair?
Who am I to lift my face up to
the warmth of the sun?

*Embody the power of the heroine
inside you,*

Envision her whole and healed.

Showing up.

Fiercely true to herself.

Loving herself.

Who am I not to smile?
Who am I not to let the gentle
breeze pick up my hair?
Who am I not to lift my face up
to the warmth of the sun?

She might want to say
Everything is just glorious, flowers
perpetually bloom, birds are singing,
and the scent of warm cookies forever
sweetens the air
She might want to say
I am fearless and without scars
nothing beats me down
But the truth is, you see, the truth is
She carved out a space for herself
  where she feels contentment more than
  she feels turmoil
She wove a nest for her little self
  where she feels safe and secure

She manifested a sanctuary for her spirit
  where she no longer apologizes for
  her brilliance
And when those black clouds appear she looks up at
them and says
  Although you might visit me you will pass
And when fear grabs her she says
  Your grip is like grasping a wisp of smoke
And when depression tries to drown her she says
  Flow through me like water and carry on,
  carry on

Artist Statement

I was a highly sensitive and empathetic child, groomed to be a people pleaser. Christianity taught me to be a good girl, to be virtuous, to be obedient, and to put other people's needs before my own. Sometimes I wonder if the combination of who I was naturally and who I was nurtured to be was a recipe for disaster.

On a special morning in December of 1973, at the age of seven, I put on my most prized piece of clothing. It was a beautiful Beatrix Potter dress with large pastel vegetables that ran the length of the dress. It felt exceptionally fancy to me. Today was going to be a magical day as I had been chosen to lead my classmates in singing "Rudolph the Red-Nosed Reindeer" at my school's Christmas program. Our families would be in attendance, although I remember that only my Nana and grandfather were able to be there.

As I walked to school with my classmates through a field covered in tall, dry grass, I was bursting with excitement and anticipation. A young man approached us on a bicycle, blocking our path, and announced he had no money and needed a nickel. In the distance, I heard the morning bell ring. All the children ran off to school. All of them, except me. I could not bear to tell the young man I had no money to give. As he climbed off his bike and crouched beside me, I discovered that it was not money he was after.

In that painful, terrifying moment, I wanted to scream for help and run, but my voice had disappeared, and my body froze. When he was done, he threatened even more harm if I told anyone. He left me like crumpled trash in that field, dirty and used. I remember hearing a blood-curdling noise as my hot, dry throat released fear and pain. Shame immediately began to bury the truth of what happened. I came up with a plan. If I hit my face, leaving red marks on my cheeks, what I could not verbalize would surely be obvious to an adult. I ran toward the school and into the office. The secretary asked me a few questions and directed me to sit on a cold plastic chair while she called my mother. My mom would not be coming to get me. I was asked to choose my lunch for the day. I chose spaghetti. Outside of the office, I walked to my classroom. Alone. I felt numb.

That afternoon, I led my classmates through the song as best I could. But absent was my enthusiasm that had shone brightly during rehearsals. While in the auditorium, I was aware of only blurry details: a Christmas tree, a piano, the echoed sounds of guests taking their seats, my heart beating so hard as I stepped front and center on the stage. I was stumbling through the hand motions I choreographed and practiced so many times, touching my nose and then using my hands to make antlers. After the performance, I begged my Nana to take me with her. Not understanding my tears, she got into her car and drove off.

From that day on, I lived in a strange dual reality of acting like I was perfectly fine when, truthfully, I was terrified and sad and alone. I had no idea that day would somehow open a door to more sexual abuse.

Today, at age 56, even after years of therapy and treatment for post-traumatic stress disorder, the events that occurred in my youth still affect me. Though now I understand that they do not define me. Creating my chapter for this project has placed me on a path toward finding my power. Every step into the dark waters of my past, I emerge a little more healed. The anger and rage that once burrowed deep inside me have been released; in their place, forgiveness and compassion grow. Two steps forward. One step back. One step forward.

CRYSTAL GASSER
BIOGRAPHY

Crystal Gasser (she/her) grew up in two places: along the Northern California coast near the redwood forest and in the mountains of southern Oregon. She has always had a love for nature and has been a seeker most of her life. She has explored a relationship with God through different sects of Christianity and has even found connection through meditation and yoga. She formed a strong bond with her former high school teacher, Kirsten Fountain, when she was eighteen. Kirsten had become a mother figure and, throughout the years, a sister and a best friend.

Crystal moved to Eugene, Oregon for ten years after graduating high school in 2010. In those ten years, while pursuing her education, she learned so much about herself. She traveled the world, found and lost love, worked, created, faced mental health struggles, and left a toxic relationship.

Today Crystal resides back home in southern Oregon, where she is currently adapting to the transition of facing her roots once again and reclaiming all the parts of herself she left behind so many years ago. This project has been one way for her to continue that work.

Blood Is Thicker Than Water

I was always searching
For somewhere to
Belong.
I didn't know that
Choosing *between*
Two creators
Would fragment
My sense of self.

They were covered
In thorns.
They poisoned
Themselves first,
Then each other.

I watched them lick
Their wounds like
Abandoned animals
Right in front of me,
As if my flesh, too,
Wasn't bleeding
In front of them.

I learned to lick
Their wounds
Before learning
To lick my own.

I am still learning to
Use the spit
And rage
Of my past as
A tourniquet to
Stop the bleeding that
Has made this life
So thick.

Flower Child

I was a child
With growing bones
And a round face.
It's true that
Most of the time
I felt small.

I tiptoed around every
Room of my life,
Studying the shapes
On the carpet,
Or the wall,
Turning the mold stains
On the leaking ceiling
Into flowers.
It was the ignorance
Without the bliss.

H*ome*
Was a variety of
Wild animals you
Should never place
Together.

Held captive
By themselves,
They barked &
Snarled &
Scratched.
They howled &
Cried.
They fought &
Slept.

I became
invisible.
This was only the start
Of a girl slowly
Learning how to
lose herself.

A Core Memory of Shame

I was with my father.
The fog was thick,
The seagulls scavenging
For a McDonald's fry.

We went inside a home
That wasn't mine.
I sat apprehensively
On the couch,
Wrapped up in my
Daisy Duck rain jacket.
I could hardly move–
Not in a stranger's home.
My body only knew
How to be still.
This was safer.

A small dog had grabbed
My attention.
I kept my hands quietly
To myself,
Waiting to be done with
Whatever business
We had being there.

When it was time to go
I stood up promptly.
The small dog's tail
Was underneath my shoe,
And all I could see
Was the end of the world.
I had failed.

The dog let out a loud yip,
A cry that pierced my
Five-year-old senses.

All eyes were on me,
And I felt it
Strong.
Maybe even
For the first time:
Unworthy.

Crying in the Back Seat

An infectious knot:
These dirty hands
Have tied & have tried
To undo.
He winds his way
Up and down
The corridor
Of my swollen throat.
A boa constrictor
Eats every last morsel
On the porcelain plate
He has made
From his own
Scaly flesh.

"I am F R A G I L E"

His eyes heavy with sadness,
Blanketed in moss
And a rust
That tastes
Just like blood.
Like an old car
In a junkie's junkyard,
He is tattered and torn.

"He is F R A G I L E"

Crack pipes and
Coca-cola stain the places
Families once sat
And drove each other mad,
Stopping at rest areas and
Then driving off of cliffs
With their children
Crying in the back seat.

Devotion

Your eyes
Were an open field
That felt like
An innocent child,
A pool of blue
Illuminated by
Sunlight.
It was a fantasy
I was willing
To participate in,
A dream that felt safe
To explore.
You were the
Keeper of the clouds,
The leader to
The veil of purple heights.
I was accustomed
To it down here,
Where my roots
Gave me the home
I always sought.
The security,
A solid ground
To dig my feet into,
In case I ever had
My world shattered
Again.

I visited the dimensions
Of your body
And your mind.
Your spirit felt
One with mine,
As we orbited
God together
Like air and earth,
Dancing ecstatically,
Always there to share

Fractal dreams
And gaze at the constellations
Of our spirit:
The blueprint of our love.

Your roots were
Shallow and yet your
Branches reached so high.
I was worried that one day
The weight of that
Would overcompensate
And we would see
The fall of Adam and Eve.
Innocent and naive
In their fantasy
Of eternal bliss.
Ignorant of the hell that
Would be revealed.
I vowed long ago
Never to let you walk there
Alone.

I traveled great depths of my
Own soul to heal.
Because our soul
Became one,
I would travel
Great depths of
Your soul
To help you heal
By showing you
Compassion,
By not letting go
Of that dream,
By trusting in all we grew
To know and understand
About a Love so rare.

Your eyes
Were a dark cave.
A lost boy within
Begging to be found,
Begging to be forgiven,
Begging to be held.
You will not be abandoned.
I will show up for you.

Like the sun shows up
Every day
For all of life,
I will be the wind you used
To know as yourself
Because I have not forgotten.
I will not forget that once
Upon a summertime
We felt like flames.
And once upon a summertime
We felt like ash.
Heaven and hell manifested itself
In the experience of our story,
And the quality of the life
We shared will destroy
Every fear I have
Of death.

Lies, Dirt, Sin

The baptismal font reminds me of Hollywood.
Neon blue, ethereal, warm and ready to adopt me.
Inviting me to become a gravedigger.
Inviting me to bury a story.

Two men, one my fiancé, wear what looks like white
pillow cases.
Dirty with sweat and tears that do not belong
to them.
Their eyes are neon blue too,
convincing.

I look down at my naked toes
Clenched and curled into the gray felt carpet,
like old nights I remember.
Like old times I am forbidden to think about.
I think about them anyway,
Until I cum back to the bishop's voice.

This time my curled toes remind me that I am dirty
and unworthy
of the house of The Lord.
Topless men dance atop the bishop's head.
He snores into the second hour, asleep at
the podium.

Broken church pews stretch for miles, infested
with seventeen-year-olds and baby wipes.
I wonder how many women here are on their periods,
and if they are ashamed of it.
My husband-to-be, with his hands folded,
burns holes into my white pillowcase of a gown.
It is stained with sweat and tears that are not
my own.

We join hands in faithful prayer,
"Dear Heavenly Father," we say in unison.

I am lying to myself here in this prison,
but it has comfy chairs and potlucks.
I am lying to myself, but it is time to go under
and let the neon blue suffocate me.

He placed his virgin hands on my bent back.
I am forgiven.
I am new.
I am *fucking* terrified.
Vulnerability never felt so good, and I descend.
Turtlenecks, canning, and skirts that weigh
dignity down.

I clench my toes just one last time,
and I go blind to a euphoria I will soon escape.

This Time Around

This time around,
My bones feel like fire.
My body is that of flame–
Too much to handle,
One could say.

I'm not sorry
For the way
I breathe,
Think,
Or feel.
Or for the miles
Feverishly walked,
For the trials
I've overcome.
Nor for the salt
Of the few
Men's tears
I have tasted.

So they, too,
Know they deserve
Compassion,
Empathy,
Love.
So they, too,
Know their tears are not weakness,
But indomitable strength.

For those I've
Given everything,
Until I had nothing
Left of myself.

So I rebuild
From the ground up,
Even stronger,
Even softer,
This time around,
This time around.

Empire of Love

Some things fall apart
So other things can
Fall into place.
Sensitivity is walked upon
By dirty feet,
Cursing women who
Feel in this world.
Telling us all
We need to wear
Our pride as armor.
Telling us that tears
Mean ~~broken~~.
I've seen them
Standing there,
Owning their stories,
Believing themselves
To be superior.
As if beyond
That mask wasn't
Somebody
With a deep wound,
Untouched.

Because here,
We use dollar bills
As tissues to wipe off
The pain.
Here, we use how fast,
And on time,
And committed
To the all-mighty
Mother *fucking* dollar we are
To measure success.

Not gratitude.

No no… here it's sink or swim.
But I'm going to remind
You all that one day
We will cease to exist

In this form
With these melodramas,
These ideas of right and wrong,
These emotions and muck.

This hard-earned work
It took to build our empires
Which will indeed crumble.

And my friend,
I hope that what does surround
You and me
In those final hours,
If they aren't stolen from us
By the uncertainty of life,
Is this:

The love-worn on the faces
Of those who have been impacted
By ~~things~~ like
Your kindness,
Your compassion,
Your honesty,
Your humility,
And your dedication
Toward being a
Decent
Human
Being
Who strives for a better future
In being good-natured
Now.

Shower Floor

Tonight I sat on the floor of the shower.
I got right in and pressed
My back against the wall,
Slid right down.
I didn't plan on getting my hair wet,
But it did anyway.
The top bun messy and imperfect.
Water droplets falling from my forehead
Onto my face.
I hugged my knees close.
Studied the bottom of the
Blue shower curtain.
The surface I sat on,
Pinkish from mildew or
Something of the sort,
All so familiar–yet this chapter of my life
Is better.
More comfortable and kind.

I've slid down shower walls before,
This time I wasn't trying to hide any tears.
But how I was reminded of the tears
I have tried to hide in the past.
The faces may have changed,
But I was the same each time.
I tried to hide from the truth,
Hide from myself,
In *that* shower,
In *that* home.
Water would fall on my skin,
I'd stare at the floor,
Unable to find rationality.
Unable to find enough courage to leave.
Unable to see the shit for what it was,
Because the idea of a better tomorrow
Always won.
The idea won, but I was losing
Myself in t(*his*) fantasy.

I was losing myself in trying to master
Unconditional love.
Until the day my face was met with real Venom and
Words that infected my psyche.

I pretend my mind is an Etch A Sketch
Some days.
Shake that shit off.
I had to amputate that life
In order to be free.
Sever it, let it unravel at the seams.
Why? Because nobody should find themselves on the
Shower floor desperate for answers.
Having to find God again because they lost sight of
What love is.

For mistaking it in some *body*
Who didn't quite know how to love back.
For thinking that my love was
Deep, or strong enough,
To pull somebody out of their suffering.
No, that is not how this works.

I'm learning.

Tonight I slid down the wall of the shower,
Greeted its floor.
My body was tired but my
Heart has never felt so full.
I rested my head on my knees,
Studied the bottom of
The blue shower curtain.
"I remember the times," I thought to myself
"The times when I was here but hiding."

I'm not hiding anymore.

A Time Traveler's Life

Early this morning
My lover shuffled out of bed
And got ready for his workday.
I tried to fall back asleep,
Instead I was focused on
The subtle change in temperature:
The cold air on my skin.
It felt frigid and crisp.
It took me back to a time
When I was younger,
Living in a dirty home,
With poor heating.
Mornings were frost,
And I contorted my body into the
Letter C,
Hugging my kneecaps to my chest
To be warmed up by my heart.

Early this morning
I traveled through time and
I wasn't wide awake.
It wasn't deep sleep.

I was somewhere in-between
Now and then,
With the same frigid kiss
Touching my now almost
Thirty-year-old skin.

I learned of a death today.
After I became more awake,
Readied myself for work,
Readied myself for the role,
Scheduled my nail appointment
Drank my iced mocha,
Scrolled the social medias,
Read the information,
That brought my body
To an absolute halt.
My skin went numb.
I set my role of the day aside,
Stepped outside,
And I cried.

I feel things, and they are sharp.
Even the softest things are sharp.
If you don't understand this,
You haven't been broken open.

A double-edged sword at times,
To experience life this fully.
But I suppose I wasn't born
To be diluted by superficiality.
I just want to say:

Holy fucking shit, we live and we die! We feel things like music,
and temperature, and love, and grief, and kindness, and holy
fucking shit—
Don't you all see how magical and heartbreakingly fragile this
all is?

But I'm afraid you'll judge me
Because I'm human, and as much
As my vulnerability is my strength
Perhaps sometimes it is also my weakness.

Late this evening while my lover
Turned to sleep,
I tickled his back with my red acrylic nails.
I held him close.

That soft and sharp feeling

Of not taking a single moment for granted.
I feel things and there is no way around that.
Instead I embrace it—
There is no other way.

I wrote a poem
Because some of us cope
With television or alcohol, drugs or sex,
Shopping, or more numbing.

I needed to keep this experience alive.
So I wrote it to share it,
And maybe you'll feel something too,
And maybe it will have been worth it.

Enough

When your awareness
Meets your roots
You will understand
The patterns and the cycles.
You will not force
What cannot
Be forced.
You will allow growth to
H A P P E N
As it should.

That doesn't always
Look like:

A self-help book,
A fancy quote,
An Instagram influencer,
Or a life coach program.

Sometimes it will look
So deeply personal
And raw,
You will grit your teeth
Trying to confront it.
It will not be
Pretty neon highlighter
We buy–overpriced–
To manipulate the chiseled
Cheekbone to nothing
Except a place to further
Hide ourselves.

But humble and bare,
Open and real as they come,
Because what is this joy
Without the real hard
M O M E N T S,
The real ugly lessons,
The painful grievances,
The disappointments,
And the reclamations,
Of choosing to embrace
All that we are?

I'm interested in this
Human-ness,
This healing,
In being
Enough.

Apartment Number 222

Two or so years ago
I made a temple in my home.
A nest to manage the deepest grief
I had ever known.
So close to this grief I was.
I tasted it each evening.
Brave streams of salt water
Made their way down to my lips
That were suddenly
Chapped and
Lonely.

I became the lit wick
Of a cheap blue candle.
I became the Ra Ma Da of
A chant that danced on my tongue.
I would stare at the art on my walls
& get lost in the constellation of pine needles.
I took refuge under a forest green Pendleton
Waiting for morning to come.

My bare feet would meet the coldness
. On the wooden floor.
The sky would match the shade of my pain.
& this is where I remembered
That even though your absence
Was a loud darkness that
Brought me to my knees,
I was also closer to my own body.
My own heartbeat.

I was in the perfect position
To pray.

If It Came Down to It

The kind of Love I want to know
Feels like the landscape of
My mind being held and honored
Like a fresh life.
Waking up to the world
Feels like my dreams
Cherished, and my power as
A woman understood deeply.
It is a power that is
Not rooted in separation   If it came down to it—
But integration.   If it came down to it—
To Nurture feels like   If
A ceremony when embracing   it
One another.   came
Like the salt   D
Of a tear dressing   O
The mouth in a promise.   W
It feels like faith   N
In each other,   to it—
In ourselves,
In humanity.   The kind of Love
It Feels like   I want to know,
Quieting the ego long enough   Feels like
To see that the kind of Love   The absence
I don't want to know   Of doubt.
Feels like possession,
Feels like lust,
Feels like *I know you*,
Feels like limitation,
Feels like I am to be submissive,
Feels like I am disposable,
Feels like I am a body before
I am a soul.

Nature's Voicemail

One sure way
To learn the
Language of nature
Is to put
Your breast to
The heart of
A tree.
Listen closely.
Tell me what
You notice
When your
Subtle body
Merges with
Your ancestor.

Do you hear
The cries?
The laughter?
The many births?
The deaths?
The beat of
Your heart
Will sync up
With the drum
Inside the center
Of the earth
And you will
Remember.
I promise,
You will
Remember.

~Ancestor

Warrioress of Light

We have nothing
To fear
In ourselves.
Not even the
Sharp voice
Of self-defeat
That comes to us
In our sleep.
For we are
Fighters
Who know
How to slay
Our own demons,
And even make
Friends with them.
The shadow
Isn't as paralyzing
When you know
You were birthed
From the promise
Of *light*.

Creator's Hands

Precious heart of mine
Know this:
In the wave
Of turbulence
You are
A glowing ember
That was born
Into the careful
Hands of *Creator*.
The moment your
Body fell to the earth
It cried,
"Mother, hold me!"
"Father, protect me!"
The flesh isn't
Perfect and the visions
You hold
Will be spoiled
In the blistering heat
Of harsh truth,
Yet *God* has held you,
For abandonment
Is not the language
Spirit speaks.

These tears,
They will flow
Into the earth.
The warm gravel
Beneath your
Bare feet will
Remind you
That you've walked
Far to get here.
When your
Demons run you
Out of town,
Away from your iced lattes,
Away from your fine and dine,
Away from your lover,
Away from your car,
Away from your tasty frosting
And your ideas
That keep you paralyzed
Or idle with selfishness...

You get to *reconnect*
With what only
A warm summer breeze,
A dip in a cold creek,
An organically grown raspberry,
A beloved barn kitten,
A cousin Terah,
And an unpolluted night sky,
Could teach you:

God is near.

Chrysalis

I am golden light,
Outstretched most of the time,
Like a sunset I've seen
Or dreamed of.
My beloved's lips
Half-open,
Eyes widened
With wonder and hopefulness.
A message in a bottle floating
To the shoreline of his iris,
Beyond the shadow of his pupil.
My body reads
Honey skin and p o e t r y.

"Embrace me,"

I whisper.

"I want to give this Love.
So stoke me
Like a blazing fire."

In my blood, there lives
A story
Of my future *family*.

This fire must be burning
If it is
To sustain,
To comfort,
To promise.
I must be *coming*
Home,
Becoming
A woman.

A code embedded
In the fabric of creation.
Why must I grow silent
When my heart beckons
To go deeper *beyond* this flesh?
A thousand petals relinquishing
Their potential.

At the moment, nature's
Clock says
S
 P
  R
   I
    N
     G.
If the heart is a portal,
I will open it
And wait for night
To fall,
For water to rise,
For tears to stain,
For flame to singe,
For dawn to dusk.

This body will
Not turn to a dry desert.
Not now.
I am blossoming.
And when I do
Withdraw,
It is only a part
Of my germination process.
I will come out of my
Chrysalis
Ready to Love
Even larger.

Meet me there.

Whole

Will the Phoenix
Swoop down fiercely?
Or the white horse
Gallop triumphantly toward
This young woman
Coming to know
Herself through
Trial by fire?
Will my lips hang
Slightly ajar,
Empty of meaning
Because I spoke
Too soon?
Am I made for
This eternal modification
Of mind?
Yes.
I ache when my Love
Has been confused
With things like
Lust,
Greed,
Selfishness,
Insecurity,
Mania,
Hysteria.

The many costumes
Of illusion.
For this Love I seek,
This Love I wish to offer,
Is a bed of roses
I make in my heart
For the beloved
To hold me and to show me
That I am already

WHOLE.

Not a hole,
Nor dirt to grow
More pain and pressure.
Not an infinite ache,
But an earth angel
Sent here
To remember this Love.
To taste it, and
To share it when it
Is ripe and recognized.

Yet this bed has
Carried a few thorns,
And I claw them out.
I continue this journey
Of purification.

Artist Statement

I first learned to self-soothe through the process of writing. I didn't have many methods of coping but the two things that kept me intact would likely be my love for nature and writing. I have a very early memory of rummaging through my grandmother's entertainment center. I was searching for a "hip" CD that I could play in my boom box. I came across a CD with a young woman on it. She had a round face and the side of her eyes turned slightly downward like mine. It read, *Pieces of You*. It was Jewel Kilcher. I knew nothing of her music, but I took that CD to my room, put it in my red boom box and pressed play. It would be safe to say that from that day forward, my life was influenced in a much deeper and more meaningful way. I began to look at things in my life more mystically and poetically.

I grew up surrounded by nature, and even amidst the chaos within the walls of my home I had a greater peace that always awaited me outside. Nature has been an enormous influence. My experimental side came out in middle school and creative writing intrigued me. Thankfully, I had a family member who was also a writer and a creative one at that. My cousin Terah (also featured in this anthology) inspired me with her raw and honest writing. Coming from the same family with similar dynamics, writing woke things up within myself that I was only (at that time) at the threshold of truly understanding. Without her influence or guidance, I wouldn't be as brave of a writer.

Writing has been about that for me: learning to brave the brutality that is life, sometimes. It has also been about leaning into the beauty that is so visceral it can change who we are if we allow it to. It has been about keeping a record of this journey so that I never abandon myself again. It has been about sharing the common thread of humanity and hoping that perhaps in some aspect of my story, another person might see themselves. It has and continues to be an ever-evolving, living, and breathing expression that I am happy to hold hands with.

KAYA MIRANDA

BIOGRAPHY

Kaya Miranda (she/her) is originally from Malibu, California, and is now located in southern Oregon. She received her bachelor of fine arts in art and works as a high school art teacher. Kaya is an artist whose focal medium lies in the field of portrait photography. Along with portraiture, she practices printmaking and ceramics. Kaya's works explore the themes of intimacy, the female form, and the male and female gaze. Her images call attention to these themes and create realistic representations of women and their bodies.

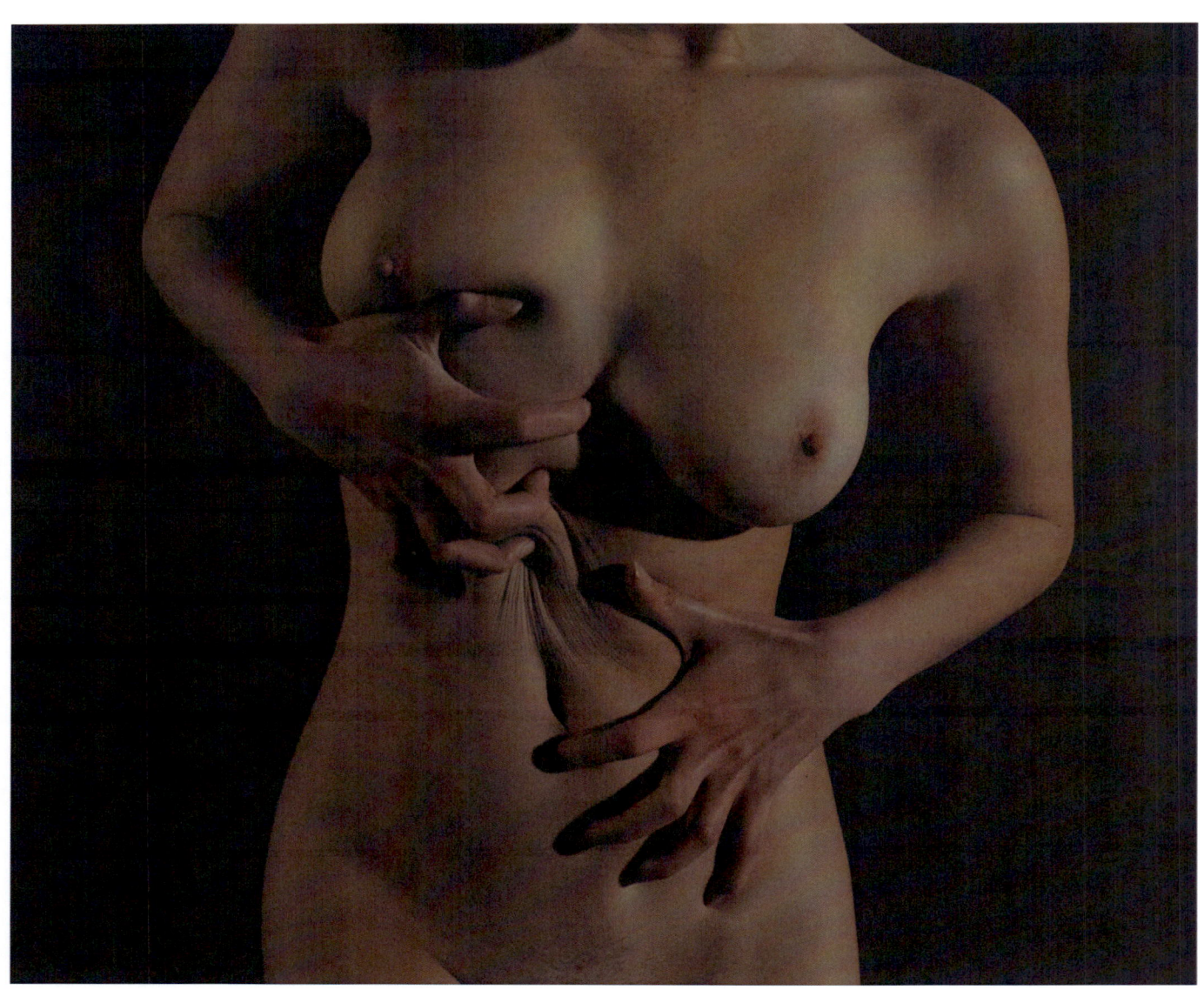

Artist Statement

As a woman, I have always struggled with self-acceptance. I have viewed myself with standards set by the male gaze: objectifying, sexualizing, and constantly judging. I subject myself to this perspective relentlessly. After years of self-torment and paralyzing shame, I began to question why and how the women I loved were unabashedly comfortable within their own skin. How did that confidence elude me? Using photography as my guide I slowly came to understand the power and beauty of the female body. The body that I had objectified and put down. The body that I convinced myself would never be good enough. Finally, I have broken free from the male gaze that has held me hostage by placing myself in front of the lens. Now I am healing, I am accepting, I am embracing my flaws as strengths, and I am replacing the male gaze with my own.

MCKENZIE LEE

BIOGRAPHY

The fifth born into a family of seven children, McKenzie Lee (she/her) was often cited as the "quiet child." Introspective and deeply feeling, she turned to music and poetry to find a way to express herself without the need to compete for airspace in her lively, boisterous home. Quietly and privately, McKenzie created a voice that would demand attention without ever needing to ask for it. Once she felt prepared to share her vocal talent, her voice became her most prized possession and her most praised gift.

McKenzie gained confidence in live performance by soloing in many school concerts and church programs beginning in elementary school. Her siblings and parents were her biggest fans, often touting her abilities and signing her up for local talent shows, even when she was too embarrassed to advertise her self-taught talent.

Life changed dramatically for 12-year-old McKenzie when she and her family moved to southern Oregon in 2003. Writing the words to her own songs became the solace she needed to get through the many challenges she and her family would face there. She continued to write her seldom-shared songs throughout middle and high school to help cope with her mother's addiction, her impossible-to-please perfectionism, and the eventual death of her mother in 2007.

Despite the heartbreaks and setbacks, McKenzie graduated as co-valedictorian in her small class of 78 students from Illinois Valley High School in 2009. She pursued a teaching career while also keeping her love for singing alive by joining one of Oregon State University's a cappella groups, Divine. Through her a cappella friend group, McKenzie met her musically gifted husband, Reilly.

After college graduation, she abandoned her teaching career to join her husband and his business partner to create music videos for well-known YouTube artists. With this acquired skill, McKenzie and Reilly soon formed their musical duo/YouTube page, The Hound + The Fox.

McKenzie, Reilly, and their children live a blessed life in southern Oregon, completely supported by their music and videos. She hopes to continue singing and writing, expand her original songwriting for other artists and herself, and share more of her creative poetry. Through her music and words, she intends to offer healing to those who may not have found their own voice yet.

Looking Out Windows

Looking out windows
I waited for you
Glued to the smudged glass
Fixated on your empty parking space

My father said goodnight
And softly suggested
I get some rest too
I didn't
I couldn't
My mother was gone
And I needed to be there
When she returned

You'd return right?
You always did

Well a version of you did
She looked different from my mother
Something about her eyes gave it away
But she had my mother's hands
My mother's hair
And my mother's soul
Seemingly trapped
Inside her unwell body

I knew you were split in two
Already at the age of six
I loved an addict
And a mother

I thought my love
Would be strong enough
To fix you
I thought my longing
Would be profound enough
To bring you home

When 3 a.m. rolled around
And her tires rolled up
I thought to myself
I did it

But I didn't
And I couldn't
My mother was gone
And all I could do
Was be there
When you returned

I Come From

I come from a white picket fence
Wood rotting on the inside
Green grass
Surrounding an oak tree

I dive to the bottom
Of the in-ground pool
The water is pristine
But the pipes are rusting
My oldest brother's small handprints
Are imprinted in the cement
(They envisioned so much more for him)

We are new here
My new friends think I'm rich
(The white picket fence is working)
We appear to be settling in
But we are running away
From dealers
Doctors
And debt

My grandfather helps us run faster
But the pace is unsustainable
And the dealers
Run here too

Privilege and I
Are no strangers
But the price of mine
Is pretending
Life is perfect
Even when I'm watching
My mother die

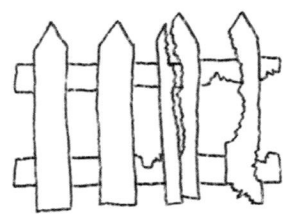

Half Full

The moon was half full
The night I was born
Split down the middle
Between the shadow
And the light
There was I
A symbol of duality
Tension
And division
I embraced my light
And shunned my darkness
I fought a war within
And thought I had conquered the night

But daylight
Is exhausting

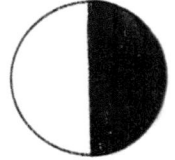

My tired cells wished for night
I slept half each day away
Only to come alive at night
And dread the imminent sunrise

In the dark
My somber songs leaked out of me
Like oil from a cracked pipe
They were messy
And left a stain

As a shadow only gets stronger in the light
So, too, did my darkness

The dueling sides of my moon
Shifted the tides
Back and forth
Light and dark

My night song
Clashed
With my day's refrain

If only I had known
How to harmonize

Inside Me

They shared a home
A mirror in my womb
Hearts reliant on each other
My heart reliant on them
I named them
Fed them
And dear God did I love them

But as many codependent things go
They could not last
As one heart stopped
So did the other
And mine stubbornly kept on beating
How dare I survive
Something so unsurvivable
How dare life go on
When death was inside me

My body has refused to move on
Stuck in a constant state of loss
Maybe something else did die within
Maybe I'm walking around half alive
With death still inside me

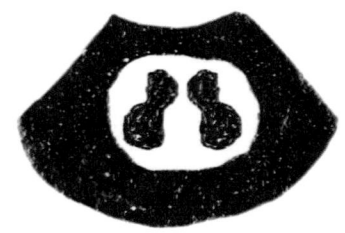

The First Stone

A priest spews his rage on the podium
A teenager in our congregation
Is pregnant
And she's starting to show

His rage is met with a man who leaves
But not before signing the cross
(Even in protest, tradition prevails)

I stand bewildered
Her parents stay silent
So do mine
She has chosen to keep the baby
And they shame her for it
He that is without sin among you
let him cast the first stone at her

At HER
They usually leave that part out
(Cunningly)

I see the hypocrisy
Crystal clear
From our single shared chalice
I taste the self-righteousness
In their tainted red wine backwash

I am fed
From the priest's hands
The body of a man
Whose teachings they falsify
I vow to unlearn the misogyny
I make a covenant
To cleanse my soul of the judgments
They tirelessly long to instill
My brain will not be washed
With their wine
I've since learned
A mind can be changed
But a body doesn't forget

So my body belongs to a church
I do not attend
My sexuality remains locked up
In their chastity belts

Even in marriage
Even for the purpose of conception
My body remembers the shame
From despicable men on pedestals
And shuts down

I respond to pleasure
With pain
And I am almost certain
This is what that priest wanted
When he threw the first stone

Internal Rot

Straight-A student
Athlete
Student Body President

There's that white picket fence
again

An addict-like obsession with my toxic
boyfriend
Excessive exercise
Binge drinking at a party

There's that internal rotting again

My public life
A flawless performance
My secret life
A dangerous ledge

I'm an incredible actor
Convincing everyone around me that
I'm thriving
I'm reckless with myself
Jumping into waterfalls that nearly pull
me under
Permanently

One September night when my abandoned heart
feels too heavy
I play a game with fate
I swerve wildly on a windy road
In a car without an airbag
My secret life
On a dangerous ledge
Almost ends
Off the edge

Adrenaline saves me
Or maybe fate
My will to survive
Turns the wheel just in time

When I return home
No one knows
Where I've been
To the ledge
They'd certainly never guess

But tomorrow there's a math test
So I sob
As I study

The next day
I'm a white picket fence again
And no one can tell
That I'm rotting

Epilogue

When children say
They are struggling
Please believe them

Weeds

What they call weeds
Flourish on my doorstep
I like the way they invite the bees
And ward off the ostentatious
There's no white picket fence here
Just a front porch full of my son's favorite sticks
Now I, too, know a good stick when I see one

There's dust on my doorstep
From our latest home improvement project
And cobwebs in the awning
(I can't bring myself to evict our spiders)

My neighbors might think we're messy
We forgot to clean up yesterday's picnic
So maybe they're right
They may say we are careless about appearances
Outside in our pajamas at noon
How can I tell them they're wrong?
Instead I wave with a smile
As a neighbor retrieves her mail

My son grows up here
Without an in-ground swimming pool
Or an acre of manicured land
He sees me learn to embrace weeds
And spiders
And judgment from those who don't understand
The difference between
A perfect home
And a happy one

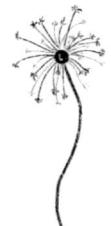

Looking in Mirrors

There you are again
A raging storm
Blowing down everything in your path
I used to hide from you
When the thunder began
It was loud and my sensitive ears
Would ring for days

And now look at me
Looking in mirrors
Seeing you

Creating my own lightning
While my son brews up his own storm

Competing for airspace
My son and I
Slowly learn
How to control the weather
Together

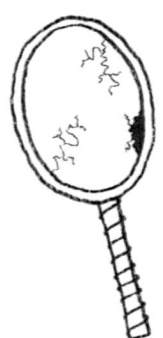

New

Twenty-four months of blood
Shedding my what-ifs
Flushing my expectations
Goodbye again, January
So long, June
These months don't stay long enough
But some days
I bleed so much
I fear I won't make it to night

Twenty-four full moons
Yet none empty
Instead we call them
New

Can I be
New
Instead of empty
Too?

Worthy

I ask my body
What do you need from me
To be good enough?
(To create life)

I rest her
I strengthen her
I therapize her
I poke her with acupuncture needles
Drown her in vitamins
And anoint her with oils

She says
Are you worthy yet?
And I say
There's still work to do

So I soak her
Massage her
Soften her
Question her
Praise her
And study her
She says
Are you worthy yet?

And I say

There's still work to do
So I test her
I give up on her
I give everything to her

I mourn her
Celebrate her
And pray for her

She says
Are you worthy yet?

I plead
What more could you possibly want from me?

She replies
For you to say
YES

A Temple

You said I was a temple
But I felt more like
A bookstore
You said no one could be let inside
But I wanted more

Is it such a sin
To be wanted?
Is it such a sin
To want?

So I locked up the windows
And I filled my moat

With fire

I turned all my pages
To fuel
And burned

My desire

Was it such a sin
To be wanted?
Was it such a sin
To want?

Is this what you wanted?
I ~~hate~~ fear
Everything about me now
I'm such a sacred place
No one in the world's allowed

I don't even go there
No one even knows where
The girl is
Who wanted

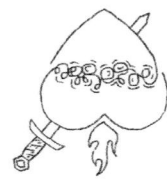

Rock Bottom

I've been trying so hard
Attempting to swim upstream
Watching on as the fish clear waterfalls
But I'm just a rock
And rocks
s
i
n
k

To the bottom I go
Heavier than everything else around me
I land
Where I've always belonged
(In bed)

The river runs over me
To places I'll never know
I stay

Through the frigid winter
To the ice-breaking spring
I endure every extreme

Nevertheless
I do endure
And when the winter returns
I now know of spring's relief
And when summer nearly dries me
I now know the promise of rain in the fall

I learn the rhythm of this river
I maybe even find comfort here
In this cycle
Of my predictable yet volatile
Home

I hardly notice
How the water's changed me
Smoothed out my rough edges
And broken down my tough exterior
I haven't moved in ages

Yet somehow I realize
Just where this water goes
And somehow I know
That's where I'm headed too

But for now I'm just a rock
And I'm right where I belong
(In bed)

—what my depression feels like

Home

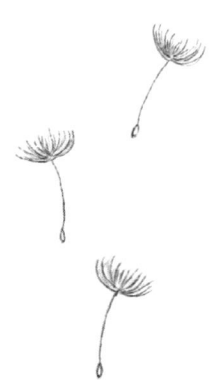

I am arriving to a home
Surrounded by forgiveness
And protected by grace
There is no perfection here
Only striving
Healing
And
Unrelenting love
We grow kindness in our garden
And acceptance falls freely from our trees

My children are safe here
To be who they are
Without fear
Or shame

My husband is blessed here
In stability
And connection

My mother is forgiven here
She rests peacefully at last

My father is welcome here
He is lighter on these floors

My brothers and sisters are healed here
They are freed from their wounds

My grandparents are beloved here
We celebrate their legacy

I am joyful here
Proud of the home
I have created

I am arriving to a home
I've always had inside of me
Where I am the creator
And the creation
Is me

For You I'll Be

For you I'll be
The mother I didn't have
A calm place
A present face
An imperfect garden
For us to grow from

For you I'll be
The mother I did have
A warrior who fought
A fallen soldier who lost
A bed of fertilized soil
For us to grow from

For you I'll be
The child I couldn't know
A safe space
A grounded place
A patched up foundation
For us to build from

For you I'll be
The child I did know
A playful dance
A limitless expanse
A mosaic tile
For us to twirl on

What Is

Each month
As I shed my what-ifs
I lean into

What is

What is here?
What is mine?
What is real?

Here is a woman
Brave enough to face failure

Mine is a family
Healed enough to not recreate our traumas

Real is a child
Loved enough to expect my attention fully

My survival guide
Is just a simple question
That I ask myself constantly

What is
Your
What is?

Outside Me

Inside me
Are entire worlds
Of words my own
Melodies are born
Through my voice
Chords vibrate
Through my fingertips

I sing children to sleep
Whom I've never met before
And sometimes I'm told they sing along
Or can't rest
Without me

Inside me
Lives hope
And possibility

My children
Both born and unborn
Continue to exist here
And as far as my voice travels

Inside me
Is life-giving-breath
Turning into sound waves
Captured for a moment
And saved for eternity

My breath
Eternally preserved
My life and theirs
Encapsulated
Existing beyond me

Even in death
My song
And theirs
Exist
Outside me

Sacred

Sacred
Too often
Means
Fragile or fleeting
Untouchable
Unattainable

But to me

Sacred
Is the dirt
From which
We blossom

Sacred
Is the rain
From which
We drink

Sacred
Is the air
From which
We breathe

Sacred
Are the moments
From which
We create

Sacred
Are the memories
From which
We learn

Sacred
Are the birthers
From whom
We come

Sacred
Are the children
From whom
We go

Sacred is
Abundant
Overflowing
Everlasting
Dependable
Effortless

Sacred is
Already here

Sacred is
Already ours

Sacred is
Already us

Over and Over

To grow a muscle
We must first injure it
We create small tears
Then let them heal

Over
And
Over
And
Over
Again

Until it becomes easier
To do what once was challenging
Then we must take on more weight
To grow the muscle once more

Those of us with many injuries
Have had to heal so many times

It seems unfair
(perhaps it is)
But look at us
Healing anyway

Over
And
Over
And
Over
Again

Until it becomes easier
To do what once was challenging
Then we take on more weight
To grow once more

Artist Statement

My poems are born when my wounds are alchemized into words on a page. Memory by memory, I am creating a new home, sometimes even a prison, for the trauma that knows no better than to reside within me. These unearthed wounds sometimes need to be locked up in ink so the cycle of passing down pain can stop with me. Words that live on paper are lighter than wounds that live in me.

Poetry, I've learned, is always honest, but it isn't always (the) truth. Releasing my raw and unfiltered words onto paper (or, more realistically, into my "Notes" app) has become a form of meditation. Without judgment, I allow the words to flow through me and bleed onto the page. Once released, I can observe, allow, and eventually let go of the stories I tell myself.

Brutal honesty is what I'm after in both my work and when I read the work of others. I want to know your deepest, dirtiest secrets and share mine with you. This is how I reject perfection and invite authenticity into my life. Come and take a seat in my darkness, my friend. Please, bring your shadow with you.

MEG BISHOP

BIOGRAPHY

Born in Portland and raised in southern Oregon, Meg Bishop (she/her) is a creator of several different art forms. She leans into the warm acceptance of her own written words and the deep connection she's always felt to music, art, and photography. Creating daily, she is inspired by the earth, kindred spirits, and simple melodies. She uses these creative outlets to help her cope with the weight that life, fibromyalgia, anxiety, and depression bring. Feeling lost in the chaos of her upbringing for most of her thirty-two years breathing, Meg is dedicating time to learning who she is, unlearning bad habits, and overcoming food addiction. She is developing healthy habits that help her both physically and mentally, both for herself and her loved ones. Meg lives an imperfectly happy, endlessly busy, love-filled life with her husband of twelve years, their two precious humans, and two fuzzy boys. Raised surrounded by mountains with every turn, their calm and graceful peaks call to her overwhelmed, introverted heart. She is a heavy-feeling, battered soul who is fulfilled most by the serenity of being alone in the company of animals and nature.

I was the one
they begged for
prayed for and more
but none of us had a clue
          what was in store

left alone inside
my darkened room
crossed my fingers hoped
    it would be morning soon

they only fought
in the dead of night
and by morning's light
        it was alright

i woke up
to cries and screaming
never knew what they were
                feeling

her lies were
smooth like butter
her body made men flutter
her love was ever-fleeting heart
        and soul never meeting

as i hugged my
stuffed puppy i walked
down the hall i held my breath
            and tried not to fall

i reached their
screams they were
muffled somehow in slow
      motion they disavowed

words
twisted
like knives
into their broken
hearts their mistakes
and brokenness stormed
              our fresh start

fists held up
high elbows back
when they were done
        eyes were black

she picked me up
and ran to the car we
drove forever but didn't
          make it far

it didn't take
long for our world
to crumble her strong
and steady walk became
a slow and weakened stumble

she locked
herself in a room
for days didn't know
when we'd see her if it
    was forever or a phase

pills and booze
were her only escape
unaware they'd leave more
                than a scrape

i was the one
they begged for
prayed for and more
but none of us had a clue
        what was in store

betrayed and alone

gone today
here tomorrow
this heart of mine
was not theirs to borrow

i begged
her not to leave
she promised not to go
she grabbed her keys said
i'll be right back my tears and
          screams too slow

i barely blinked
while she drove away
with a man i didn't know
          head half bald
                    hair gray

we were
alone just dad
and i we cried and
cried until our tears ran
dry with nothing left hearts
felt broken i laid in his arms
          words went unspoken

tossed like
a rag doll between
hundreds of miles the houses i
lived in could line up in aisles

groom
after groom
bride after bride
they took their marriages
                    without stride

each one's
heart more broken
than the last each partner
on both sides lost connection
                              fast

each marriage
brought fighting
each fight brought
          hurting

repeat
   leave
     repeat
       leave
         repeat

each partner
hurt me in their
own special way
each partner gave
me something to say

one said
i was a liar
i was going to
hell for my sins
one told me to get
out this was his house
                    i was living in

one said
i was lazy and
made up all my pain
she quickly tuned me out
          when i tried to explain

one caused
a fight i tried to
run and hide he punched
a hole right through a door
where she was on the other side

they all left
they all yelled
they all took a piece
of me i now have to meld

[part one]

i sat
quietly
in the back
seat of his car
as we drove to a
place that wasn't very
                far
we picked
up two women
they sat next to me
and then we drove again
      to a place i couldn't see

nothing but darkness
surrounded us now our
bodies bare and cold i tried
                to disallow
they said
it will be over
soon just sit back
and relax so I closed
my eyes while fingers
touched and they finished
                up their acts
he was
sitting in the
front seat watching
from behind it didn't take
long until our bodies were entwined

once he
was almost
finished he climbed
into the back i remember
i felt sticky i felt gross i felt bad

he finally
crossed the
finish line i was
paralyzed with fear
i silently cried and wondered
            why am i even here

parts taken

[part two]

she said she'd
show me hers if i showed
                her mine
i exposed
myself and
her sister walked
in but instead of running
            she had a grin

what was
meant to be
curious quickly
turned injurious when
her older sister walked in

months went
by and it continued
my heart and body fully
                nude

the sister watched
the sister used force
not an ounce of regret
      or a bit of remorse

all of my
skin felt like
needles and pins
when i was with the
            sister who grins

words of destruction

sticks and stones
may break my bones
but your words they will
destroy me forgetting that
i still existed with each sip you
     took to be free

you took
a sip of poison
to try and numb
the pain but once
you took the first one
you failed to stop again

it was during
those times it seems
all hell broke loose and
when i'd try to pull away it
 was me you would accuse

you said that
i was worthless
wouldn't amount
to much and said that
i was a piece of shit because
    i didn't do as such

which normally
meant i stopped
taking calls from you
because every time i answered
     i'd get abused

words of
destruction
screamed into
my ear words of
destruction were all
    i could hear

every time
i tried to leave
you pulled me back
somehow even as i write
this i wonder *what are you*
    doing now

what i
saw before
me each time
i saw your face
a vision of the pain
you caused locked within
                    a case

all the
children
that you
damaged
because you
wouldn't control
the urge you didn't
stop to think what could
                    possibly emerge

creature

you blamed
it on the drugs
and in the past it
happened to you why
is it when our souls are
hurting we hurt others to
                    feel renewed

i could feel
your poison
when you looked
into my eyes the way
your urges called to me
        was really no surprise

within

i witnessed
the feeling of
innocence broken
it sent me into a spiral
for all the words unspoken

from all
the children
you groomed
and carried through
dirty tasks to all the people
who fell for all your many masks

i saw you
looking back
at me when i looked
into the mirror melding
with the poison is what i
                    always feared

unalive

willing
vulnerability
was never my
forte it burned to
put my feelings out
     for display

the world
could surely
see the darkness
that was inside i spent
my entire life trying to hide

can i go now
i would beg and
plead i didn't want
to be here i just wanted
     to bleed

i sliced
myself until
i saw red attempting
to cut the thoughts out
     of my head

i didn't
want to be
here the pain
too much to carry
and all the words i
had left to say were
     easier to bury

all i
felt was
darkness
surrounding
my tender heart
i would have rather
ended it than go back
     to the start
when
instead
of living you
try to just survive
that's when your soul
is crying and feels most
     unalive

art is healing

with a
pencil in
hand i erase
this painful feeling
and drift into a place
    of artistic dreaming

with a
clean slate
of paper cleansing
my painful past i choose
to feel this feeling and know
            that it won't last

my mind
begins to quiet
swaying my hand
without a fear embracing
this artistic dreamer whenever
                she is here

all
the pain
is gone for
now a distant
shadow in its place
a reminder of what's still
to come of what i haven't
                faced

these curves
along the paper
this pencil in my hand
give me strength to face
the pain and try to take a stand

as i learn
to control the
story that is flowing
out of me with each choice
that i am making i know i can
                set me free

lost and alone

when wind
blows through
the trees the branches
wave hello reminding me
i'm on this path the one that
　　　　helps me grow

as clear
as i am part
of earth and it
a part of me these
parts of me i could not
　　find now i finally see

in all
its twisted
vines entwined
in their own embrace
i find comfort in this knowing
　　i'm allowed to take up space

with
thousands
of colored petals
imperfectly aligned
reminding me my flaws
don't need to be confined

like fallen
leaves that
crumble until
they learn to grow
again i'm learning to
grow from the pain with
　　　　every count to ten

water
renews my
body helping
me survive breathing
in the forest is where my
　　　　body thrives

with each
mountain i am
given i hike up to
the top with each step
i keep on growing and i
　　　　never intend to stop

when all
you feel is
body aching
when all your
limbs will not stop
              shaking

when every
day your weakened
mind surrounds with fog
            it's hard to find

when you
sleep all night
and wake up tired
or can't sleep at all
because your brain is
            wired

when insanity
is at your door
with legs so weak
   you're on the floor

when you
struggle with
intimacy because
it feels like a sin with a
corrupted mind that can't
            look at bare skin

this is
when you
realize the pain
they caused will
            never die

the pressure
of his body was
sure to cause some pain
it feels almost unbearable to
            stand up straight again

i blocked
him out for
so long but now
i finally see the pressure
he forever imprinted into me

the pain
that i am feeling
can't be seen by the
naked eye without this
representation you couldn't
                  if you tried

that's why
all the doctors
kept turning me
away *you're too young
to have this illness* is all that
                  they would say

after time
felt wasted
and i began to
give up hope a very
special doctor took a step
            on this steep slope

answering and
confirming what i
knew for so damn
long so many answered
questions so many proven
                  wrong

i can feel it
throbbing and
burning through
my skin if fibro truly
showed you all my pain
you'd finally see the pain
                  i'm in

parts given

prisoner of inside

these thoughts
like weapons inside
my head from all of the
evil things that were said

what makes
you think you
deserve to be a
mother you will be
a terrible one why even
         bother?

you will
hurt them
like i've hurt
you and there
is not a single thing
    that you can do

this love
won't last
just wait and
see don't you
know you're just
        like me

shut your
mouth and
close your eyes
no one buys your
      pitiful cries

are you sure
you need that extra
bite your stomach size
       says otherwise

tied to
the pain these
thoughts can bring
makes breathing feel
      like a sharp sting

it hurts
to breathe
it hurts to think
drowning in thoughts
      i quickly sink

all i want
is to be enough
for myself and for them
all i want are these thoughts
    to stop but it's myself i do
          condemn

misplaced within

suffering
to stay consistent
with every step i take
when all i've known is
brokenness it's easier to
                    fake

but *fake it*
'til you make it
will only get you
so far if you keep
it up forever it's sure
        to leave a scar

struggling
with commitment
throughout my entire
life between all the broken
promises and lies that felt like
                    knives

the everlasting
betrayal that this
curse has put on me
makes following through
with anything feel like i can't
                    breathe

despite the
million thoughts
that never go away
i choose to fight for
t h e m i choose to stay

desperate to
give them a l l
the life that they
deserve this love
i have for t h e m
is forever preserved

i didn't
know me
before t h e y
came along it was
t h e m who gave me
the courage i needed to
                    be strong

i step into
the darkness
i didn't want to
see i step into all
the parts that make
me   me

i know
down inside
i have so much
pain that could hurt
those i love but that's
why i'm trying to heal and
why they've been sent from
                    above

i try to be
someone who
isn't blind to who
i am it wasn't until
t h e m i was ready
    ready to take a stand

afraid of
the abandoned
little girl that's inside
t h e y brought her out
when she wanted to hide

i want to be
better for all of us
i want to know me and
to love me would be a plus

i'll make
mistakes and
keep doing so
t h e i r effortless love
        helping me grow

my love
for t h e m
and t h e i r s for me
continues to nurture and
                set us all free

like the
wings of an
eagle soaring through
the sky i ask *who am I*

growing

together
we've been
in the depths
of despair with
hearts that were
broken from things
        that weren't fair

thinking the
cuts drugs and
boys would heal us
thinking we'd leave the
earth behind without a fuss

but we held
on tightly through
it all we held each other
up when the other would fall

you've
been there
through thick
and thin never
knowing when the
healing would truly
                begin

little did
we know in
the midst of the
storms is when strength
        and healing truly forms

Best
you inspire
me with your grace
and elegance with your
beauty wit and eloquence

you stand
up proud with
all you are no matter
the pain or bruises or scars

the pain
they've caused
can't take us together
the bond we have being
        too strong to wither

you've loved
me for me and
i've loved you for
you from the day that
we met it's like we just knew

best friends
forever is what
we've always been
bounded soul sisters
from beginning to end

together
we're in this
with your family
and mine this is your
time this is my time this
                is o u r time

i've got you
and you've got
me g r o w i n g
together is where i
    forever want to be

more than a feeling

memories linked
the good with the bad
the ones that made me
happy the ones that made
        me sad

entwined
within each
other i can see
it all so clear they
both needed the other
while the other would steer

to experience
life to grow from
the hard to embrace
the small things to be alive
      though scarred

to be
inspired
by life and
all that's within
even the pain has
purpose when i really
      dive in

to healing
that pain and
taking back my
life letting go of the
past that holds all the
      strife

my birth
mother she
holds me with
pure love and intention
i squeeze her back with
    reciprocal affection

she never
wanted to let
me go she knew
she had to let me
      grow

to keep me
safe from harm's
way she knew we'd
find our way back someday

my momma
she loves me
and i love her back
she fills the empty spots
    where others still lack

this bond
is so natural
beautiful and true
knowing she's there
when each day is through

i am more
than the feelings
that are flooding inside
i know i am safe now and
    don't need to hide

free and alone

freedom
for me is a
feeling it's the
feeling of being
found the feeling
of sun on my bare
skin while i cannot
            hear a sound

the feeling
i get when i
daydream of a
simple homestead
with trees away from
the hustle and bustle to
live with the birds and the
                        bees

freedom
for me is the
spark i feel deep
down in my chest
when hearing a sweet
tune or melody that makes
            me feel my best

it's letting
go of all that
has ailed me i've
grown from my past
and my pain the feeling
i get when i'm happy running
            out to dance in the rain

freedom
for me is a
feeling one i
have finally found
there's still work to be
done here and i see freedom
            when i look around

parts strengthened

little drops
all in a row
upon the grass
   ready to grow

trees
stripped
bare down to
the core knowing
this makes them better
           than before

some flowers
fade in the dead
of the night knowing
others will bloom against
         the cold fight

the earth
it knows just
what it needs no
doubting or fearing
   it just believes

it knows
that to grow
you must face
the storms then
let it all go with wide
       open arms

facing the
past will never
be easy but it's
part of this life if
i want to live f r e e l y

i didn't
want to face
it i did everything
but try the pain was
too much to carry i didn't
       want to cry

i've now
faced the wild
storms of the past
not knowing how long
  this journey would last

but here
i am on the
other side my
inner child will no
       longer hide

the parts
that were t a k e n
i fill them with love gently
releasing the pain to above

the parts
that were g i v e n
i treat them with care
i rest when it's needed
and breathe the fresh air

i'll move
with the wind
and learn from the
tree that stands in one
place but still seems so free

when parts have
been taken and given too
i strengthen these parts as a
    commitment to y o u

unraveling of captivity

these thoughts
that hold me captive
i lay them down to rest
unraveling each layer that
        puts me to the test

i'm no longer
victim to the poisoned
thoughts inside as each
passes through me i choose
        to be their guide

thoughts
and feelings
are ever-fleeting
just breathe and they
go by like a passing car before
        me or a bird up in the sky

i know
it's never
easy when
that first step
feels miles away
but to start unraveling
the captivity i let them pass
        and sway

they aren't
here to harm
me i can choose
the path they take
i am safe here in this
moment i choose the path
        i make

found within

daughter
sister   aunt
friend   wife
mother until the
                    end

these are
the titles that
you all can see
they mean so much
but there is more to me

now that i
can see who
i really am i can
be who i am and not
            give a damn

i may have
rough edges
i still have a lot
to learn but i stand
tall with pride at how
            i have turned

i am
strong
but gentle
honest and kind
forgiving but smart
with an empath's mind

i try to
grow from
my mistakes
i'm teaching my
introvert not to be
                    fake

i thrive
in nature
in the calm
and quiet feeling
and noticing everything
    flowing within the riot

for noticing
the little things
means beautiful things
too like the sun on my skin
            the fog and the dew

the birds
that are flying
from one tree to
another noticing how
they support one another

i am loving
compassionate
understanding of most
creative and thoughtful
    completely engrossed

in the dreams
i have for myself
and f a m i l y this
is just a glimpse inside
                of me

looking
around at
the beauty
earth can give
fills every piece
of me that makes
    me want to live

i look
again my
heart starts
racing at all i
could've lost had
i listened to the aching

embracing
what makes
me feel alive
makes my soul
      truly thrive

taking flight
i join the birds
letting go of painful
         words

i fight
for this
imperfect
life i choose
to put down the
    mental knife

i'm done
being my worst
enemy now that
    i am finally
        f r e e

Artist Statement

When you've never looked inside something, how do you know what's in there? You know there's something, but looking might change your life completely. It might change your entire being. It might hurt. When pain is confronted with the willpower to heal, it begins to diminish. Maybe not fully, but it will try to. Especially if you let it. From birth, unable to live with my biological parents due to my father's sexual abuse both within and outside of our immediate family, I was adopted within our large family of aunts and uncles to ensure I would be p r o t e c t e d. They all held a big meeting regarding who would take and raise me up as their own while still allowing my birth momma to have a relationship with me. For this, I am so grateful.

I was argued over. Begged for. Wanted. Loved. Then I was placed with two very broken souls who had good intentions: my uncle and his wife. Their marriages, both together and separately, were a big part of my undoing as well as part of shaping me into the person I stand here proud of today. I tend to easily lose sight of the importance of living because of the hardships I have and still continue to face. With this chapter, I am learning to g r o w from the hardships and pain, trying to become the best version of myself I can be, while embracing who I am now.

As I untie and unveil the trauma that wraps me up in its ever so beautifully battered blanket, I use poetry and imagery to represent both the beauty and the wreckage of this life. Starting from some of my first memories, flowing through to the life I long for, each word is entwined with a rhythm that sets out to create an atmosphere of vulnerable, artistic apprehension for the reader of my story; one that leads to an overall knowledge of who I was, am, and want to be.

Being invisible is where I've always been more comfortable. I guess you can call this the empathetic introvert in me. I didn't want to be seen. I didn't want to be heard. I barely wanted to breathe to ensure nothing I did hurt a n y o n e. Including me. Especially me. For I was my own worst enemy. Reliving my past, finding my present, and seeking my possible have been life-changing. Writing and creating this chapter has helped me heal in ways that are changing my perspective of myself, my loved ones, and life itself. I am ready to be seen. I am ready to be heard. I am ready to b r e a t h e. Knowing through this, I am healed enough to (try) to stop myself from hurting anyone. Including me. I am looking for the beauty in the small, precious moments here and now. I am trying to embrace the flaws and imperfections with the pain because they are important and beautiful.

I am too.
I am m e.
I am M E G.

JC SMITH
BIOGRAPHY

JC Smith (she/her) comes from a long line of warrior women; they have always been strong, innovative, and courageous. One of her great-grandmas used to ride a Harley and worked at Boeing during World War II, riveting her family's way to financial stability. Another great-grandma, emigrating from San Salvador to San Francisco, could see a dress in a store window and come home to sew an exact replica by hand. Yet another grandma raised seven children while getting her PhD. She became a professor of women's studies, religion, and philosophy, as well as an artist and an author. JC's closest grandma has nurtured her dreams from the first time their eyes met when she was born. And JC's mom has impressed the power of inquiry, creativity, and intuition on her through nurturing her passionate pursuits of knowledge and innovative feats.

From caring tirelessly for aging mothers, to passing down traditions of delicacies, to going to whatever lengths necessary to protect their children, the women in her family are remarkable beings. They have been homemakers, teachers, librarians, waitresses, secretaries, laborers, writers, fighters, and lovers. JC has idolized every one of them and is proud to have followed in their footsteps—their legacies have laid her life's foundation.

While this foundation has been bonded with love, resilience, and strength, it has been also cemented with as many hardships; they have all had to endure abuse, addiction, codependency, depression, poverty, and suicide—many of them more than one of these. However, if it were not for these rocky roads and potholes, they would never have the fulfilling lives that they have lived and the ability to build resiliency and provide strength for those around them.

JC Smith dreamed of being an educator from an early age, and she eagerly pursued that dream right after high school. She now works and resides in Oregon's beautiful Illinois Valley. In addition to teaching and learning from her students, she is also constantly amazed by the life and love lessons of her greatest teachers, her two children.

Little Lane

I come from
a little lane lined with tall pines
and taller cedars and vines
and the rotting corpses
of old cars and trucks decaying alongside
the burnt dreams of past ambitions

Inside the sagging exterior (with a strong foundation)
of our tiny house (it had so much potential)
and underlying the potent smell of onions and beans
lingers the stench of cheap wine and cigarette smoke
and darkness
and backed up septic
and sink drain
The sounds of incessant commercials and wordless
chatter permeate the tiny space
emanating from the constantly blaring TV
Violent storms and angry tirades
and the whacks of the belt on bare skin
add to the din

My dreams keep whispering

The skeleton of the living room walls (devoid of
paneling after a long-ago remodeling whim)
is stuffed with peeling silver insulation reflecting the
dim light of the lamps
dulled further by grey clouds of smoke and
resignation

My dreams are quietly stirring in the shadows

I share my bedroom with the washer and dryer
heated when the laundry needed drying
venting into my room
No Scotch tape sticks to the walls
posters sagging

My dreams are hanging on

Mom puts on a strong front
barely making ends meet for us all
hiding money
hiding pills

Allotting only so much for the rotgut
and our away games
and school clothes

She knew
She knew to kick down the door and grab the rifle
before he put his toe to the trigger

The second time she wasn't fast enough

I was already gone
by then
That day
I walked across the stage
lined with professors and flashing cameras and bright
dreams and full-fledged fires of ambition

My dreams long gone from that little lane

What if...?

How is it? you'd ask with a slur
Night Train in a coffee mug, cigarette burning
We frowned, rolled our eyes
Slurped up your delicacies
Good
Mmmhh
Fine
We'd all reply without feeling
Going back for seconds, and sometimes thirds
You'd add, *well, it must be good if you want more*
Uh-huh
Yep
It's good, Dad
Thanks
I told you I would take care of you

We changed our name back
Chose the name of a father we barely knew
No thought for you
Only because we were old enough
To understand with you
Understand the addiction
Hear the slur
Took out our anger on you
Our abandonment
You on us

Reciprocal hate
Round and round
You said you would take care of us
Out you went
No thought for us
Only for yourself

Why is it still so hard to believe?
Why do I still ask "what if?"

What if we had lavished you with praise?
What if we had told you how much
We really loved your meals?
Your music?
What if we had kept your name?
What if we all hadn't been so angry?
What if we had known how much you cared?
What if we knew now what we didn't know then?
What if we could tell you right now
Our best memories of you?

What if we had known that you needed to hear
them?

If only I had given you that letter I wrote you when
You were finally clean and sober for a while
(I read it at your funeral)
Would it have made a difference?
Would I be able to tell you all that was unsaid?
Would it have been any better?
For you?
For us?
For what?

What if?

Broken Mirror

Reflecting fragments
Of the past
Repeated fissures

C

    R

        A

                C

        K

  S

S M A S H E D

With wicked words
Again
And
Again
Reverberating

Selfish
Fucked up
Evil bitch

Loud through these walls
Tunnels through time
Smelling of rotten wine,
Beer, and hatred
Dripping with loathing
Spilling to the floor
Splashes of red
Wiped away
To be spilled
Again
And
Again
Fractions of the past
Returning with every crimson crack

I N

                S A N

   I T Y

Brushed under the rug

Fantasy

I must admit the pangs I get
Of jealousy, fear, and regret
Every time I see
A couple treating each other with courtesy
With respect and love
With what we all deserve
No mockery, no competition
No constant degradation

Every time I hear
Of a family wanting to be near
To each other without having to fear
That anger's ugly head will rear
Spitting fiery words dripping
With disgust and loathing
Constantly berating
Constantly humiliating

Breaking
Me
You
Us
Down

What once was family
Has become a fantasy
A distant reality
That I can only barely see

Peace is rare
Inevitably, anger comes to tear
Ripping, shredding the threads to pieces
The negative cloud never ceases

Tearing
Me
You
Us
Down

What have we become?
Can our past be undone?
"For better or for worse" we pledged
But we are right on the edge

Pulling
Me
You
Us
Down

I long for your embrace
A kind word, a smile on your face
I miss the man you were
Calmer, kinder, gentler
I want the father you can be
I want us to be a real family
Full of love, trust, and positivity
Fun, laughter, and true prosperity
Is it too much of a dream?
I want that fantasy

Not Lonely

I dance alone
Arms open to the music
Feet pounding
In rhythm
With my heart
Alone

It is only
me
I am
alone
I have
always
been alone
I am the only
one
that I count on
It has
always
been that way

I have given myself
let myself be known
truly known
raw

open
my deepest temples explored
embraced for a time

Dancing entwined
I felt safe
This is love, I thought
This is how it should be

I should be able to lean on someone
Be vulnerable
Be open
Be me

But that self, that being, is
Yet again
Twisted to seem selfish
Warped to seem unfair
Torn to seem apart
Unfit
Unmoved

I *am* a part
I *am* re moved
I am me
I dance alone
By My Self
Again
Always
Alone
Only me
But not lonely

Empty

One rice cake—breakfast
(dry)
One-quarter of a sandwich—lunch
(half is too much)
Just one bite
Just enough
Conveniently absent for dinner

Are you hungry?
No, thank you.
I already ate.

You swallowed WHOLE this illusion of power
You are FULL of self-criticism
GORGED with imperfections
Devouring every delicious pang

STARVED
For control
(out of control)
CRAVING control
(being controlled)

Face is gaunt
Sucked up
Legs too thin
Ass is gone
No tits
Ribs sticking out
Hip bones protruding
Size 0
Perfect

Perfectly
E
M
P
T
Y
And still powerless

Home

I come from
a long winding path
of curiosity and exploration.
My foundation was built
out of stones of love,
beauty, and support—
and legacies of warrior women.
The walls had been haphazardly
put together—
boards of experiences tough
and enlightening—
nailed together flimsily in places
with self-doubt, fear,
and lack of self-control.
In others, they were studded
tight with resolve and
growing confidence.

My walls are now stronger—
reinforced with self-love
and strength.
My dreams whisper through these walls,
past, present, and possible.
Through the many windows
of all shapes and sizes,
light shines from within
and without.

My maze of rooms of memories
continues to be built,
adding large expansive suites,
tiny secret closets,
and hidden rooms,
full of treasures,
some brilliant and some dark.

The high steepled roof
has been strengthened
over time
to withstand the storms.
I stand tall—
weathered by the elements,
yet
sheltered by love and light—
embracing the days
and the nights.
I am home.

To My Children

What will you remember most, my son?
Will you remember all the times we laughed?
Or all the times you cried?
Our mad morning rushes—words flown without
thought?
Our calm afternoons?
Our nighttime chats?
Thoughtful discussions?
Questions, ponderings, and lots of love?
Or will you remember the pain?
The years I kept us there—
The years you had to hear the hatred?
Directed at you?
At me?
What have I instilled upon you?
Love and openness,
Or frustration and anger?
What will you remember, my son?
What will you take with you?
Who will you become?
I will always be here for you.

And to you my daughter,
What will you remember most?
Our giggles and silliness?
Divulging our dreams?
Or the frustration and rage?
Who will you become?
What can I do to help you be your best You?
I constantly question what have I done,
To make you this way?
How can I uproot the seeds of ire,
Of helplessness,
As you have watched and
Listened to the rage around us?
How can I help to instead sow seeds of peace?
How can I nurture your energy and
Beautiful spirit?
Cultivate creative space for you?
I embrace ALL of you.
I will always be here for you.

I will never let you go.
You are my heart.

I am forced to face the worst in myself,
Yet also allowed to face the best in myself.
I give you both my best.
May that be what you remember most.

A Way

A lone goose
cries out to open sky.
Her mate has lost his
way.

She peers back
through the stormy clouds,
but she cannot quite
pinpoint where they parted
ways.

Looking forward,
gliding softly,
she lands on open water.
The future rippling peacefully
reflects promise on this new
way.

Design

As my eyes pore through
her beauty surrounding me,
the greens, blues, and grays,
her sounds echo from the hillside.
The birds   all around,
The frog   on my right,
The bug   in my ear,
And pull   my attention.
Here I am,   she calls.
What was I looking for?
I ask myself.
A sign, I suppose,
Of her hand   in mine.
My heart calls;   my mind reaches.
I am your sign,
kisses the wind.
She takes my hand,
once again.
Here, child.
I am always here,
as she dances by.
She embraces my heart,
eases my mind
Don't fear;
simply, don't forget me.
I am you.

(Un)Tethered

This freedom is an illusion
I am still tethered
Still chained
By our souls' thread

It is knotted and drawing
Tighter
Strangling with every
Tug
Every pull

Yanked from my blissful
"Freedom"
Reminded of the connection
Wound tighter

A little slack here
Pulled again taut

Needing to be severed
Let to fly
Finally

Untethered

Finding true freedom
My new reality

Grounded again
Brought down
Back to reality
Still tethered

Enough!

Purge the illusion of
Powerlessness
Starve the lack of
Control
Don't feed this farce anymore

We are enough!
Good enough
Strong enough
Brave enough
To say
We've had
Enough!

We have inhaled flying fists
We have tasted oceans of salty tears
We have bitten back screams of violation
We have choked on violence
Oozing through
Generations
Threatening to swallow
Me too

Enough!
Stand up
Take control
Realize our power
We've had
Enough!
We have
Power
We are
Em*power*ed
We are more than
E
N
O
U
G
H!

Versos Soñados | Divine Verses

Versos Soñados

Yo soy una mujer compleja
Con pensamientos profundos,
Y antes de morirme voy a
Conocer a otros mundos.

Yo vengo de la locura,
Y hacia la paz yo voy:
Busco la belleza pura
Para encontrar bien quien soy.

Yo sé que no sé mucho:
Más hay que siempre aprender.
Y aún cuando sepa algo,
Sé que ya me va a cambiar.

Yo he visto las tormentas
En hogares y afuera,
Y sale de las cenizas
El amor escapando la ira.

Vi crecer la resiliencia
De la fecundidad de la vida,
Y vi nacer la creencia
De poder dejar la pérdida.

Yo sé abrirme al cielo
Que me entre la brisa fresca,
Y en un nuevo camino
Me enfrento lo que aparezca.

Yo sueño con el aire libre
Borrando tanto dolor;
En la profundidad confío
Abierta a la luz del amor.

Divine Verse

I am a woman of depth
Always pensive and pondering,
And before this life's death
I plan on much wandering.

I come from insanity,
And towards peace I strive:
I search always for beauty
And my true path in this life.

I know that there's much I don't know:
There is always more to learn.
Every day I change and grow;
For enlightenment I yearn.

I have seen the storms' destruction
Both outside and inside these walls,
Yet emerging from the demolition
Love escapes and hatred falls.

I saw the resilience grow
Out of the fecundity of life:
I've seen as belief is sown
That love lives through strife.

I know to open myself to the sky
And let in the fresh breeze;
On this new path I fly
Able to move forward with ease.

I dream of the air so light
Erasing the painful past;
In the eternal I confide
Open to the love that will last.

This poem is written in the spirit of *Versos Sencillos*, by Cuba's revolutionary poet, José Martí. I wrote it first in Spanish, and then translated with rhyme and meter to mostly mirror the original meaning.

Bathed in Moonlight

Your gentle features
Aglow from moonbeams
And from within
Your inner light
Shining brightly
Even dreaming
For now, you sleep
At peace
Bathed in moonlight
I will take care of you always   What is your dream?

Then, your hands, your feet
Reach out
Searching for comfort   It is possible
Your fingers latch on to mine   That
Calming quietly   You
Reassured with this simple dreamy connection   Are
Again, you sleep   The
At peace   One
Bathed in moonlight   To
I will take care of you always   Break
                                                   This
I write these words   Cycle
Awash in moonbeams
And your special glow
At peace
Bathed in moonlight
I will take care of you always

For now
So young
So innocent
So strong

A Little Branch

I saw a little branch stuck in the river.
Reaching from the dark, turbulent depths,
Another branch held it at bay.
The little branch swayed in the rushing water,
Almost breaking free.
It seemed to be waiting for the water to rise,
A little bit more,
Waiting for the flood that would wash it clear.

Back and forth it went with the ripples,
Sometimes almost free.
Yet as much as the little branch seemed
To yearn for escape,
It was also safe in the familiar grip of the other—
Fearing what awaited downstream.

The rain started pouring torrentially.
The stormy waters roiled past,
Threatening the safety of the little branch,
But allowing a drink of the fresh waters ahead.

Finally, the river rose,
And, snapping from the dark depths,
I saw both branches break free.
Still, the little branch clung on;
Needing the security,
But also relishing in the newfound freedom—
Flowing quickly on.

The rains and flooding began to subside,
And the two branches finally parted.
As they went around the next bend,
I saw them floating
Side by side.

Wise Warrior Woman

From the Womb
From Within
Shining light   *fiercely reverberating*
Intertwining heartstrings   *lovingly embracing*
Infinitely connecting
The web of all
That was, that is
That will be
Wise Warrior Woman

Primal cries   *in the night*
Guttural screams   *in your dreams*
Deep eyes   *wells of wisdom*
Laughter and pain   *stream out*
From Your Soul
From Within

Echoes of our Earth Mother
Exploding with colors
In every shade
Your brilliant soul
Never losing light

Another rotation
From Light to Dark
From Spark to Spirit
Wise
Warrior
Woman

Life Dancer

Twirls and whirls
Spins and turns
Back and forth
Fast and slow
Step close
In stride
Dips and jumps
Ballet toes
And do-si-dos
Breaks and taps
Constantly in motion
Painful and beautiful
Mesmerizing and energizing
Round and round
In step
Count of eight
Infinite
I am a Dance Divine

Full

I am hungry for life
Craving all the delicious morsels
That every day brings

Savory or Spicy
Sweet or Sour
I want them all

Every
Single
Crumb

Every
Tiny
Scrap

Letting go of
The need for control
Allowing the grand mystery
To prepare my plate
Content without
Criticism
Pleased with
Imperfections

My body has birthed two beautiful babies
My breasts have nourished their little lives
My arms have carried us to new possibilities
My heart has opened with joy and wonderment

I am full of love
Devouring every moment
Perfectly imperfect
Perfectly
F   U   L   L

Artist Statement

I write to record my journey, however flawed or unfinished. As expressions of the strong emotions that fight to be heard, my words give life to my feelings; ranging from short rhymes to extended metaphors, from lyrical to haphazard, poetry embodies my life's trials and triumphs.

Despite many dark detours (I don't know where, or who, I would've been if I'd stayed on any of those unlit side trails), these diversions have colored who I am today. My past poetry paints those pictures. At this current lighted juncture, I know that every step I have taken—be it clumsy, surefooted, backward, or sideways—has landed me in this promising present full of possibilities.

I hold no grudges, no resentment, no guilt about my past. I have learned that we can only do our best at any given time, and I give my all at all times, whatever that might look like. I have found my power through poetry, my confidence in sharing, my raw reality in revelation.

This is me.

I am emPOWERed.

ABIGAIL SPENCER

BIOGRAPHY

Abigail Spencer (she/her) stands grateful, having lived many lives encapsulated into only thirty-three years. Abigail's experience of family changed drastically when she was three years old. She watched as her mother found partnership with another woman and as her father found a new partner. Because of her non-traditional family, Abigail began experiencing an incredible amount of judgment and bullying from the kids at the Catholic school she had to call home for seven years, as well as the neighborhood children raised with the same values as the previous generation. Abigail felt alone.

She grew older and a little less wise as those closest to her floated in and out of her life, leaving only agony, debt, and remnants of multifarious drugs in the rubble. The path chosen and paved for Abigail led her to an attempt to flee from the generational trauma bred inside her home. In running, she ran into the arms of the same things she was fleeing from: momentary "love" given and equally taken from her in toxic exchanges. When Abigail turned seventeen, she met her first husband and celebrated her first month of sobriety since she was thirteen years old.

She was soon married to a soldier, living in Hawaii with their beautiful son after suffering continuous miscarriages; all seemed right, if not at least a little better. Alas, there was so much more in store for her. After years of vicissitudes, their life together ended in divorce. Abigail traveled back home to Grants Pass, Oregon, with her son. Grateful for pain, raw and sordid growth, she stood in it.

Cradling her child, she met "light" in the form of a man who provided freedom, friendship, and unconditional love. That man continues, to this day, to be the support of a profound shift in Abigail's life. They celebrated their love by bringing another healthy baby into the world to accompany their son. They continue their partnership while collaborating with her ex-husband in co-raising their son. After all, Abigail believes there can never be too much love.

Eighteen years clean, Abigail continues to relish in it all. The reality. The truth. The wholehearted madness and love. The joy and the grief that live so closely together. And so much damn growth.

So many lives lived in such a short time, and it's just the beginning for her. Continuing her journey, Abigail is intensely dedicated to her husband, her spiritual relationship, two rainbow children, a deep passion for photography and writing, and her growing career in the financial industry. Abigail intentionally celebrates that she is alive to live this many lives, all encapsulated into one.

Bound

bound and blinded is where i stood
breathing in toxicity stemmed from misplaced intentions
generation to generation it was passed down
and i stood in it
lungs full of dreams that lived far away
remembering **them** and their words
bruises drawn in a beautiful shade of blue
like the ocean **flooding** my mind
confusion was key so i wouldn't catch on
not allowing questions or second thoughts
every day was a fresh start for you
never for **me**
these scars have been living on my skin
each time you speak **deeply digging in**
every time i feel stronger
you put your sights on me for longer
bound and blinded is where i stood

Smothered

Gasping

gasping in this beautiful place
expensive china
carefully set out
each hand-selected item to fill **your** home
pieces of me hand-picked
but not placed so delicately on the shelves to view
unspoken　tucked away　hidden
i was not for viewing
gasping in this beautiful place
where breathing did not come naturally
yet **refashioning** me was second nature
learning at a young age
watching from the back of a
long　dark　hallway
of your home
practicing to become just like you
one day maybe you'll place **me** out and love me too
gasping in this beautiful place

Hidden

Dirty

dirty and **he** made me that way
i laid on the musty couch
eyes on the cartoon playing while his touch **was**
upon me
dirty and he made me that way
i laid on the concrete city ground in the snow
eyes on the changing streetlights
praying red made him *stop*
dirty and i made me that way
i laid on the bed time after time
eyes on the soon to be forgotten face
only to be a vague memory
dirty and i was made this way

Overcome

Tears so big   I am so small

Bound

i am bound to the path
i **must** move forward
equally frozen and warm
i will break the pattern
as i feel the blood that runs through me
this sits with me
it ran in the family until it ran into me
and i stand
after running over the rocks that sliced my
feet
through the fog that circles through my
mind
remembering them
their words
the excuses i made
the way i held myself
it will all be okay
a reminder that i am alive
i am bound to this path
glimpses continue to haunt deep within
this time my feet are hard
the path is worn
i **stand**
holding the little girl who has now grown
we are bound to this path

Smothered

Gasping

gasping in this beautiful place
the mountains outlined carefully with fog
sunshine outlining each scar upon my skin
defining me and every truth that is unraveling currently
there is no place to be hidden as my naked body
feels **the** breath of the wind
i was made for viewing
gasping in this **beautiful** place
where breathing comes naturally and i hold myself gently
i have stepped out of the long dark hallway of your rules
and i am venturing into my own **unknown**
not knowing what the future holds but knowing right now
i am
gasping in this beautiful place

Hidden

Dirty

dirty and i make me that way
i **fight** my way through a self-waged war
eyes upon the life i so **desperately** seek
dirty and i make me that way
i dig my way **through** the versions of me that
i find to be too big or too small
dirty and i make me that way
i unlearn what i have been taught but **the**
days
carry
on
and on they will go until i lie cold in the **dirt**
dirty and i make me that way

Overcome

Forest so big   Worries so small

Bound

bound by the rush of truth
breathing out the past and **nurturing** the parts that still bleed
we are not naïve to the evils of this world
in pretty dresses and pearls
vividly remembering them and their words
the bruises once drawn have sweetly left their shadows
a reminder of what can be easily passed on to
the **innocence** we have left and have birthed
and though we stand in the midst of trepidation
we allow questions and second thoughts
every day is be a fresh start for me
for the person who traveled a thousand worlds with me
this is just the beginning
bound by the rush of **truth**

Smothered

Gasping

gasping in this **beautiful** place
dancing in the **freedom** of self-given power
with each hand-selected item i've put in my home
pieces of me hand-picked
placed delicately on the shelves to view
not unspoken　　　not tucked away　　　not hidden
*my life was made **for viewing***
my pain for all to see
gasping in this beautiful place
where i have worked endlessly to breathe
unlearning what i learned at a young age
practicing to become anything but like you
one day maybe you'll place me out and love me too
come what may
i have placed myself out to view
i am
gasping in this beautiful place

Hidden

Dirty

dirty and he made me that way
i will fight through the words swimming in my head from
previous lovers wanted and not
yet he fights too
dirty and he made me that way
the day the stars aligned he came with a rag in hand
washing away the fear instilled by another's touch
dirty although we made me that way
seemingly to never go **away**
i rewrite the last chapter of my book
the one i thought was already set in stone
you can only clean something
dirty
and we made me that way

Overcome

Heart is content　　I conquered all

Artist Statement

Have you ever opened your mouth, only to realize that you are shackled by such emotion that you cannot physically use your voice? You are left completely and utterly paralyzed, and you are certain that you could fall to the ground at that moment because surely it isn't normal to feel something that intensely.

My biography provides a brief overview of just a few defining moments that have left me literally speechless, and it doesn't begin to touch the trauma. Through the years, I have found that when my body is struck in such a way that I cannot possibly utter a word, I find my voice through photography and writing.

I can stand so high on the top of a mountain that I fought to climb, feel the mist fall from the fog that dances above my head, and bask in all the beautiful glory that only nature can provide. Then I take a picture. An image that forever captures the wet, heavy evergreens that barely swing as the wind attempts to consume them. Yet, they stand tall and mighty. I can take a picture of the soil mixed with jagged rocks and new seedling growth. I capture it all with my camera, cohabitating.

That picture speaks to the freedom I have fought for, the recurrent abuse I no longer suffer, the trauma I am still recovering from, and the children I am raising differently than I was raised. It speaks it all.

It speaks to the goosebumps on my skin and the wind upon my lips as I capture its vast beauty. I can stand alone at the top of that mountain and breathe in the crisp, clean air, cleansing the dirtiness inside of me. And when I go home to the comfort of my now very safe home, I can pull up that photo and relive it all over again—finding a new beautiful thing with each gaze—my goal: cohabiting with joy and grief. The art says it all when I cannot.

TERAH VAN DUSEN

BIOGRAPHY

Terah Van Dusen (she/her) was raised by her father in a small cabin. It was there that she learned to appreciate the lost art of silence, reading, and the spiritual satisfaction of a simple walk in the woods. Raised as an only child, her creativity was nurtured during the long, agenda-less days that stretched out before her. She considers herself fortunate to have lived a childhood so completely wild and free.

But carefree her childhood was not. And when Terah began writing autobiographical poetry as an adolescent, she never stopped. Today Terah is the author of four self-published books of poetry. Her personal essays and poems have appeared in multiple print and online literary magazines. She writes about connectedness with nature, spirituality, the complexities of family and relationships, motherhood, grief and loss, and her unconventional upbringing off-grid in Northern California.

When not writing, Terah runs a farm with her husband and daughter, outside of Eugene, Oregon. She can often be found ankle-deep in manure, contemplating her next story.

Picture Day

The little girl in the school photo
has blue eyes that will soon darken to hazel
pinstripe black eyebrows and brunette
hair that tumbles past her shoulders
her bangs are cut blunt and a little uneven

What you see is the gentle smile of a six-year-old

What you don't see is the girl carefully selecting
her school clothes in the morning
a red dress with a white lace collar

What you don't see is her picking them out of
a small neatly folded pile at the foot of her bed
in a room shared with her father on a family farm

What you don't see is that for the past month
since they'd relocated to the farm
the girl in the red dress with the white lace collar
and the baby teeth who was learning to
spell words like cat and cross was also
navigating daily a geriatric sexual
predator with whom she shared a
last name

Most people look at their school photos and
laugh at their out-of-date hairstyle
I just see a tortured little girl

I want so badly to reach out
and hold her heart
to keep it from breaking

Origins

I come from
the end of a short
gravel road
fifteen miles from
the nearest grocery store

Dad planted six fruit
trees when he bought
the property
he told me five of them
were mine

Today, a fifth-wheel sits where
my dream bedroom
was going to go

I can still picture
the window of the
imaginary loft bedroom I sketched
in my notebook pad using no. 2 pencils
Dad sharpened with a pocket knife

When we go to see him now,
we camp down the road, by the river
I play with my toddler in the sand
the same sand where I used to bury treasure
with the neighborhood boy, Johnny
right upstream from where I got sucked down
into an unforgiving whirlpool,
twice

I build fire
carry water
by the river
I come from
a place
not a town
more like a speck
of water
on the map than a dot

Almost

I don't know how many others
woke without their mothers
but I'm sure there are a few
out there

As a child
I was notified by the hum of the engine
idling in the drive that it was time for school
fog hanging in the evergreen mountains outside as
Dad readied himself for work and me for my day
small, simple acts of care that sometimes resulted
in mismatched socks or field trip permission slips
forgotten on the kitchen table, next to the kerosene lantern

But for every action missed by her, Dad was there with two:
two kisses atop my head when dropping me off at school
double the attention on my birthday, twice as much Halloween candy
a big kid, Dad was double the fun

It almost made up for her absence
almost

Mother

Can you hear me now?
Can you hear me now?
Can you hear me now?
Can you hear me now?
Can you hear me now?
Can you hear me now?
Can you hear me now?
Can you hear me now?
Can you hear me now?
Can you hear me now?
Can you hear me now?
Can you hear me now?
Can you hear me now?
Can you hear me now?
Can you hear me now?
Can you hear me now?
Can you hear me now?
Can you hear me now?
Can you hear me now?

1996

I hear
her mother
whispering in the hall
We can't afford to keep
feeding her
I know
I should tip-toe
out the back door
past the clothesline
and around the corner
I'm mad enough to do so
embarrassed
a motherless little girl
getting on my best friend's
mother's last nerve
but I am hungry and
haven't had a thing
all day
the mother turns up
the television
so that I can't hear
and when my friend comes
into the bedroom
looking concerned
she says
I'll just share my food with you
she knows me well
enough to know
that I was listening
through the door
Whatever, I say
as my stomach growls

Out of some sort
of courtesy
I leave

I smoke cigarettes out of
an ashtray back home
it's a trend I keep up for
twenty years
but now people
come to my house
for dinner
and even though
I can't afford to
keep feeding them,
I do

Not So Hot

Too easily offended
I'd rather not listen
to some people
most of the time
My anger is my
downfall and rage
follows, like falling
boulders, from behind
I'm antsy in my heart
which the doctors have
confirmed–they say my
heart doesn't pitter-patter
right

Some days are fine
some nights are worse
some are best for not
speaking at all
but I faux smile
cause that's what
people want of me
it's what we want
of each other

Silence is threatening
and often misunderstood
only meditative if you're
…drinking hot tea before or
…wearing lycra and a yellow
scarf with elephants on it

I lie on the bed
or I cry
because I can't feel my head
like a hot air balloon it has risen
and escaped me
no longer attached by way of
my spine to my feet
no longer accepting responsibility
for foul thoughts and behaviors
truths I've built up with strong
hard-to-destruct things like
addiction and the inability to
see love clearly
the tendency to judge love

inspect it for faults and errors
I beg with my body but
sometimes
I do not give it up when he comes
for me
when he is ready

When he is ready I sometimes
see the hands of another man
a man that some of us women
know all too well
the very hands of a man
who first showed us hell
who turned an ordinary meadow
into a
red burning thing
where all routes leading out
only lead to more traps
and catastrophes
the hands of a man
can either help or threaten me
the hands of a man
can trigger me in the best
and the worst of ways
I'd say don't come for me on
a day like today

I'd say don't come for me
I'd say my devil man hands
never paid
as many of them don't
too many wrists, unroped
so many women coping daily
in millions of different little ways
I myself
toxify
detoxify
toxify
detoxify

Inside my mind I am
wringing my hands I am
pulling my hair I am
opening my mouth
to scream

my eyes are bulging
out my pretty little head
I am coming apart at
the seams
and though I can't
seem to get a grip
                    I am still

And all I am actually doing
is leaning on the stovetop
and staring at a boiling pot with
hot salted water and chicken

One would assume
I am daydreaming
thinking of nothing
blank

But I am a poet
and I am still scared in
millions of different little ways

I am still scared in the way that
too many grains of weightless
sand could crush my every last
bone like the way a toddler
could drown in half a
bucket of water

I am still scared in the way that
teenager held her breath and her
friend pushed on her chest and
she died but it was all supposed to
be a joke
an experiment

My anger has turned to sadness
My rage into despair
Some things
many things
are too difficult
to bear

Act of Forgiveness

My single act of forgiveness includes
doing something I once heard he would do
he would drink one glass of water
for every cup of coffee

coffee
water
coffee
water

Quite calculating
this one small act of self-care
coming from a man who
plucked futures from
little girls like me

Sabotaging as he was
when I drink water
with my coffee
I forgive him

It's the only act
of forgiveness
I will allow

How High?

How high must I get?
Must I touch the sky?
Fondle the clouds?
Burn my fingertips
on the sun like
a child would do?
Didn't I learn the first
time I touched a hot
burning thing?

How high must I get?
Must I balloon?
Must I get so high
it hurts when I fall?

How high must I get?
Must I get high beyond
my problems?
High enough to point
and laugh at the mess
I've made of myself?

How high must I get?
Does life need to be a
psychedelic plaything?
Does life need to be a joke?

Third Eye

Pulse
pulse
numb
numb
I navigate
moment-to-moment
day-by-day
in and out of
different states of consciousness
I am alive
I am f
    a
      d
        i
          n
            g

I am both
dis   connected
and whole
yin and yang
but you won't hear me complain
about this tortured state-of-being

Human Being

Because if underneath it all
I am not in pain
in my body
then I have as many blessings
as there are stars in the galaxy

If I am not suffering
I can
and should
bow to the floor in grace
resting my forehead on the floor
third eye crushing into the wood

There is something
so grounding
about it to me

To feel
the tempo
of the earth
on my third eye
to calm my tortured
state-of-being

Human Being

Moonbeam

My single act of forgiveness includes
piercing my right ear four times
and my left ear three
every wince a memory
of her

My Mom
Moonbeam
the free spirit who wouldn't
stick around

…for long
A woman too young
too wounded herself
to know how to manage
her firstborn

…me

My mimic
these seven earrings
my single act of forgiveness
one piercing for every hole she
has pierced in her pale earlobes

Because deep down I want to be
something like her

                    My Mother

I just don't know which parts
I want to adopt

This sterling silver, a symbol of love
and my second single act of forgiveness

Camellia

You don't know it yet
but the hiding place you
called the rose tree
is really a camellia bush

Its hearty pink blooms will
always remind you of the monster
you were escaping

In the springtime, even thirty
years later, the camellia bush
brings to mind his harmonica
on the shelf
his rock collection
on the windowsill
and his touch

Within those pink petals
you see the complete lack
of justice
scot-free
and you sit with
that sadness almost daily

But the farm will sell
and your great-grandfather
will die in a mental institution
because he fondled too many nurses
at the old folks' home

You do not know it yet
but you will find the courage
to write about the rose tree
about gripping its hearty branches
about getting up high
and out-of-reach
and how everyone acted
like nothing happened

You don't know it yet but
          they didn't know
          they just didn't know

You do not know it yet
but you will finally unbind yourself
from any shame because…wisdom helps
and you understand that the word shame
belongs to the abuser
not the innocent being
the Human Being
whose trust was
kidnapped

You do not know it yet
but others will rise
and others will write
and
that will
make the journey
more comfortable
more acceptable
more forgiving

You do not know it yet
but the hiding place you
called the rose tree
is really a camellia bush

Its hearty pink blooms will
always remind you of the monster
you were escaping
and the beauty that
was there all along

Free Spirit

I used to be confused about
what a free spirit was

I thought it was the ability
to break off, to sever

completely from vulnerability
…from a lover or a problem

maybe eye around on the bottom of a
bottle or a baggie for the solution

maybe Kate Moss about
cigarette dangling from my lips

expressing myself from my hips
not giving too much or too little

I thought it was not needing a friend
I thought it was tethered to the high, to the wild

and then I realized
that true free spirits don't need a thing to be free

don't need a drink to be funny
don't need a pill to be sexy

don't need a smoke or a toke
to take them in and out of the moment

I realized that true free spirits
are unattached from all of that

unattached from insecurities that drive us to looking
outside instead of inside where the peace resides

Emerging

I need to find my endings
so that new stories can

                  e   m   e   r   g   e

Transformation is strong
and alchemy is at the
root of my creativity
Through writing
we transform our
experiences
we hold them
we own them
we claim them
we design
our past, present
and futures

I am calling in endings
to my stories
like the one
where I am all alone

I want to write a new
story where I am supported
loved, cherished, and understood

Because the world needs
our beautiful,
our messy,
our true,
our light,
our dark,
our deepest and wildest words
I need to find my endings
so that new stories can

                  e   m   e   r   g   e

Kaleidoscope

I am keeping it real
I am keeping it simple
I am following my intuition
and my intuition is grounded
in a real sense of direction
I am kindness over coolness

I am not questioning
my own authority
not anymore
I am letting loose into creation
I am taking the dirt of my
experiences
spitting and making clay of it
I am shaping of my
experiences
a bowl to contain them all
like how our skin
is just a vessel
for our stories

I will shrine it
I will stow it away
I will never forget
certain moments of
certain days
I watch my life
as if on stage
a wall-leaning observer
a sometimes orchestrator
a container of both chaos
and order
this body, solid
this mind, wanderlusting
this spirit, pulsing

I observe the play of
night and day
the come and go
of the tides
the movement
of the planets
and the moon

I walk through the
quaking aspen
I sit under the
weeping willow
I settle, at last
in a redwood grove
I am growing
taller
stronger
and supported

I bring my palms
into prayer
I stop
I stare
a kaleidoscope of
living and breathing
all around me
I fold into myself
and just breathe

I let go
I grow
I breathe

Let go
grow
breathe

let go
grow
breathe

let go
grow
breathe

let go
grow
breathe

let go

grow

breathe

The Magical Mundane

Look for the blessings
look *hard* for the blessings
do not be self-centered
do not be self-boasting

For all that you take
give, give, give
love your daughter beyond
your definition of it
love, love, love

Rejoice

Somehow,
step-by-step
make the mundane
magical

Remember the
lessons of your
ancestors

They went something
like this:
smile
even when in disagreement
but speak your opinion
and let it be known
avoid passive-aggressiveness
it serves no decent purpose
make the next best choice
if you have it in you

Shower or bathe
put on a dress
or a pair of muck boots
whatever the moment calls for
make your little life list:
these are the mundane things
that bring me magic

Begin again

Take care of your
little universe
best you can

Blossom

This is how it feels
when I believe in myself:

It's not always very graceful
though I wish that it were
it feels *true* though
it feels hot pink
and sparkling
like I am a flute
of rosé or a glass of
chardonnay

It feels sober though
as if I'm heading in the
exact right direction
it feels like what I want,
need, and deserve

It feels like a
vista before me
as if I am seeing my life
for the very first time

It feels like I am a bud
then a blossom
then it feels like
I am blooming

My Girl

27 ½ pounds of
giggly joy
smile bursting
with a gap-toothed grin
buttery palm smacking
my eye socket
because she doesn't yet
know nice touch vs. not nice touch
my shock dissipating into love
her love fueling my every action
thought and decision
27 ½ pounds of
Autumn:
full-faced
freckled
and
flawless
My Girl
at age 33
I was finally
so ready to receive her!

Marigolds and What It Takes

Because I am a survivor
I am in a perpetual
state of self-care

Today,
I impulsively
bought one dozen
marigolds

I was so afraid
of losing footing

I imagined the flowers
in the sunshine, light filtering
through their tangerine petals

Hope, in the form of fresh-cut flowers

Anything to keep the
memories away

Last week
I tinctured myself
back to sanity
peppermint
and patchouli

The week
before that
it was
red wine in
a stemless glass

(I didn't always take
good care this way)

But if only it
were as easy as
buying a thing

It takes
the thinking
the positive thoughts
it takes
the purging
the negative ones
it takes the turning over
of the stones

All of them

It takes the believing
just as I did today
that the radio deejay played
Dylan's version of "House Carpenter"
and his song "Simple Twist of Fate"
back-to-back just for me

It takes the being selfish
it takes the being unselfish

It takes the breathing in
it takes the blowing out

It takes whatever it takes
rock and roll, church
to bring me back again

Today I bought
one dozen
marigolds

I imagined the flowers
in the sunshine, light filtering
through their tangerine petals

Hope, in the form of fresh-cut flowers

Artist Statement

I write first and foremost for myself. Because unless I write, I don't feel good about myself. Maybe, after all these decades, it's just what I'm used to. It's where my worth lives. I also write to pass on that indescribable feeling when you read something that makes you feel so heard, seen, and connected that you're elated for days afterward. My writing doesn't aim to end on a positive note, it aims to end on a truthful note. It aims to land where the story actually landed, after I've massaged an idea for years, and marinated it beyond belief, in an effort to find its core meaning. I write to connect to the deepest parts of myself and share that feeling or mood with others. I read to do the same. When I write, although it is personal writing, it feels more like I am channeling something bigger than me.

In my twenty years of writing, I have come to understand its importance is so much more than coming up with a story. Writing is an act of rebellion. It is a form of protest. In many cases, it is a path to justice or redemption. It can mean liberation. Through writing and publishing, we all possess an inherent power. Think of all the underprivileged, abused, and silenced among us. Then imagine reading a book and gaining their perspective. With courage, we humans can set our own stories straight.

The classic diary is such a symbol of hope. It can be used as a nonviolent weapon to combat assaults of all kinds. When I was abused as a child, pages of my diary were later photocopied and used as evidence in court. So now I believe that every eleven-year-old should have a diary. If they're fortunate, those pages will contain innocent descriptions of a carefree childhood. If they're unfortunate, I want them to know that those same blank pages can carry them home to themselves, and become literal records of their truths. There is nothing more intimate than a story. For better or for worse. Although I've found it's almost always for the better.

KAIDEN VALENZUELA

BIOGRAPHY

Kaiden Valenzuela (they/them) was born and raised in southern Oregon. They received their bachelor of fine arts and are now pursuing a career as an educator and freelance artist. Kaiden's art practice consists of painting and drawing, with a focus on acrylic, watercolor, and colored pencil mediums. Through their work, they investigate different mental states represented by narratives and symbolic figures. Creating art as an autistic person, they view their work as a way to connect with others in a way that expands beyond verbal language. It is within this space that the true self is revealed, outside of our bodies and deep within our minds. They hope to meet you there.

Kill What Kills You

What is Missing

Excision

Root Wound

Riding the River of Fire

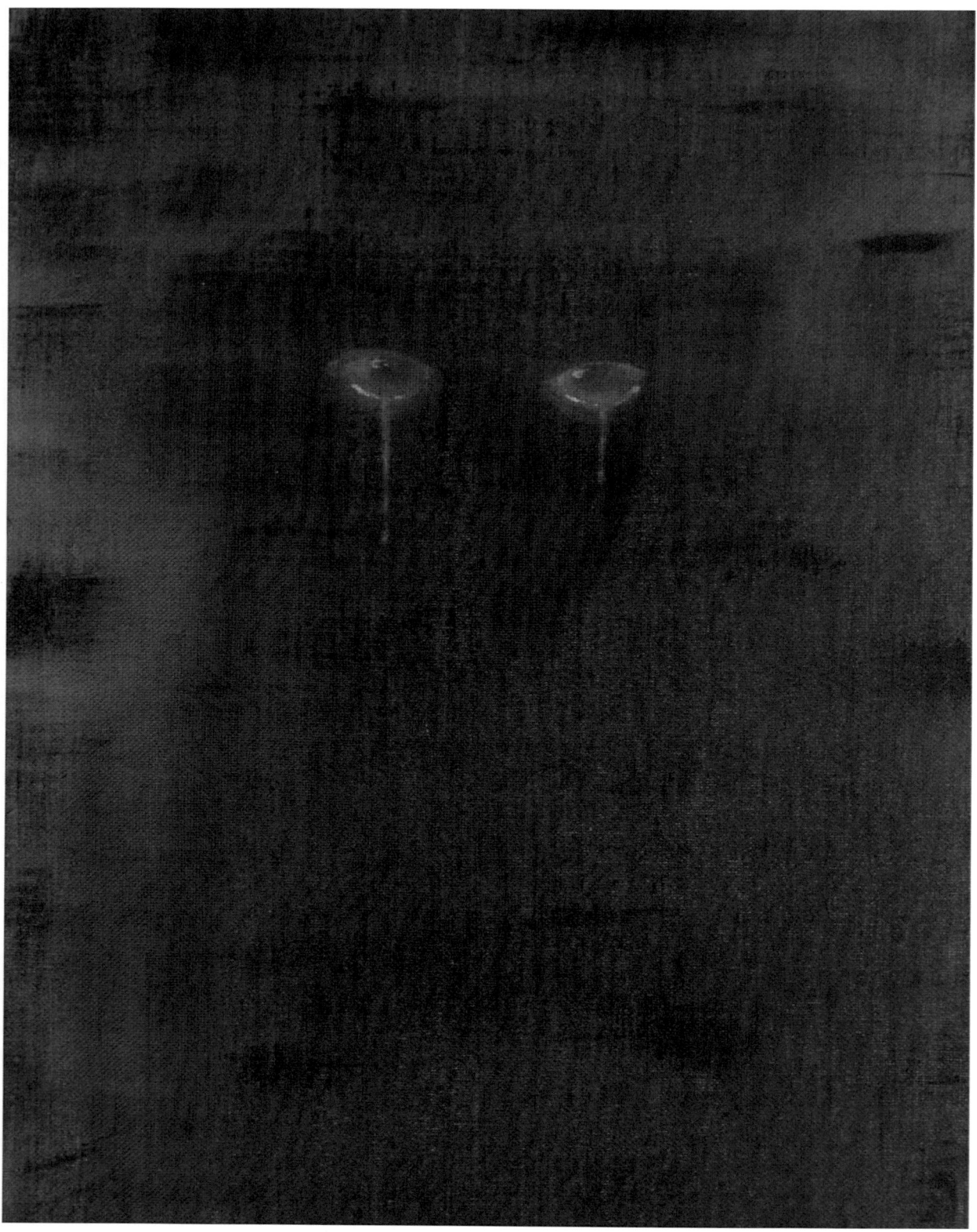

Beneath

On Nights Like These

Love, Hate, Fear, and the Self

Romantic Encounter

Journey to Self-Love pt. 1

Journey to Self-Love pt. 2

Forever Home

Ovule

Endless Cycle of Pain and Joy

Fairy Birth

Homage to 'The General Zapped an Angel'
By Karel Thole

Actualization

Font of Creativity

Artist Statement

"I Am All of Me" is a collection of works that uses both representational and abstracted landscape self-portraits to examine and exhibit aspects of myself and my past that I find difficult to explain with words. In lieu of the taxing and vulnerable nature of verbal conversation, I create visual narratives that capture my traumas, secrets, and moments of self-reflection. These paintings explore situations of anxiety and despair, the subject presented in an ambivalent state between life and death, their pain unfolding in a frozen, precarious moment. It is within these pieces that I allow myself to reveal my ideations and fantasies of letting go while simultaneously, viciously, proving that I am alive within the act of creation.

I want to tell you so badly, but that would be too easy.

Wouldn't it?

BIOGRAPHY

Kirsten Fountain (she/her) wholeheartedly taught middle school and high school social studies for sixteen of her twenty-six years as a passionate educator. She then transitioned to instructional coaching and professional development, first for her school district and later for multiple districts in her region.

Like her grandmother and mother before her, being an educator is a part of who she is, and she is so much more. Above all, Kirsten is a connector. She understands that each person is talented and creative in their own unique way and seeks to discover how to encourage those she loves to cultivate their unique gifts in service of their growth.

Kirsten is currently curating a life filled with love, connection, and care in a cozy cottage in beautiful southern Oregon with her soulmate, Tim, and their three cuddly cats. She is now focusing full-time on healing physically, emotionally, and spiritually after a lifetime of codependency, perfectionism, shame spirals, anxiety, and various health impacts of complex PTSD resulting from childhood abandonment and abuse. Poetry and photography, along with therapy, have been keys to unlocking her healing. She has the honor and joy of being the mother of Kaiden, the child who became her greatest gift and teacher. Kirsten was thrilled and humbled that Kaiden joined her on this healing journey, creating the chapter prior to her own. They continue to heal together with unconditional love and grace.

Origins

I come from
An anguished
Discussion of divorce
Across the table
Upon which I sat

My chubby toddler hands
Reaching out
To grasp their own
Uniting them
One by one
Atop the other
Then sealing them
With a pat

A fading figure
Finding freedom
Freeing his children
For the taking

A rosebush-lined drive
Deep crimson and thorns
Receiving
Releasing

The scent of peach cobbler
Soothing with
Sweetness and spice

A pear orchard
Dotted with asparagus
White blossoms
Smudge pots
Hope and
Overwhelming isolation

An old abandoned train car
Mysterious
Beckoning
A whole world to explore

Within those
Red
Rusty
Walls

A garden bursting with life
Weeds constantly threaten
Knees and hands dirty
With daily defending

A barn owl hooting
A diligent
Constant
Protector

One nest containing
Two invaluable eggs
Vulnerable

A looming
Omnipresent
Paralyzing
Weight:
Terror

Sweet weaponized words
Spiced with poison
Released
Received

A whistling white belt
Bruising
More than our bodies
Scarring
More than our minds

A savior
Our mother

A diligent
Constant
Protector
Taking flight

A new nest
Carefully
Compassionately
Constructed
For two invaluable
Vulnerable
Sisters

Free

Safe
At
Last

The Feeding

The River of Life
Flowing through my veins
Is tainted

Rotting

Delivering
Shame
Blame
A thousand-million lies

Feeding my soul
A constant diet:
Death

Fear
Is
Here

Shame throws the door open
Trumpets blare
Every cell in my body
Braces
Prepares

Screaming with glee
Fear
Tears into me

My ears
Heart
Brain
Guts

Fill with sensations that
Burn
Break
Bloat
Cut

Bleeding
Bleeding

Pleading
Pleading

The reservoir fills
Drowning me

Hell

I succumb

When I gather the strength
To rise once more

Again
It comes

Unbidden
Unwelcome
Symbiotic

Keeping each other alive
Just enough to

Feast
Once
More

~~Authenticity~~

To Whom it May Concern,

No
I haven't seen
[felt]
[done]
[heard]
[lived]
what you have.

Yet,
I know what you need.
I define your success.

I decide
if you fit
[and where]
[and when]
[and how]
[and why].

Conform,
bend,
become
[like me].

We don't have room
for authenticity
[you].

Warm regards,

Your Family
[Friends]
[Partners]
[Church]
[School]
[Employer]
[Government]
[Dominant Culture]

O No

The most intimate part of me was
Wrapped in caution tape
Loudly insisting
"DO NOT CROSS"

I had been told
So many stories
Filled with
Horror
Death
Destruction
Disease
Infestation
Loss

"WARNING! DO NOT ENTER"

At first
I was convinced
It must be evil
I didn't allow myself to
Touch the opening
Part the curtains
Or
Peak
Inside

So
I made myself some rules
That's what good Christians do

I wouldn't touch it
Neither could anyone else
Sacred is as sacred
Does[n't]

Then
Passion
Replaced fear

I discovered that
The tape was
Removable
Flimsy
Replaceable[!]

We
Entered
Together

We explored it all
Except one room
You know
The Big O[ne]

I couldn't
Betray my mother
Betray my grandmother
Betray my church
Betray my Self

I didn't
I don't

I locked the door from the
Inside

I remain
Outside
Carefully
Replacing
The tape

Vacuum

When I told you
I loved you
I meant
"I need you"

I
NEED
YOU

My black hole
Of a heart
Didn't know the difference

My very existence
Depended
On your
Body
Heart
Mind
Soul
FEEDING
My own

I
Consumed
You

I couldn't comprehend why
We
Both
Perished

Dinner for One

I sat for
A meal
Longed for
All my life

Shared between
Life partners
Absent
From living

Instead
I ate
My words

Consumed
My hopes

Masticated
My dreams

In silence

My plate

full

My life

E   M   P   T   Y

Tough [to] Love

Are you okay?

Asked a hundred times a day
What I really need to know is
Am I okay?

This is Codependency		To cut this cord I must ask myself *Am I okay?*
This is Childhood trauma	This is Me	And stay right there
This is Being highly sensitive	Tied to You	Holding my [little girl] self Loving my [little girl] self
This is Self-defense		Comforting my [little girl] self
This is Vigilance		Saving my [little girl] self Until I finally receive an Embodied response from My Core Self

I am okay

Love²

When two people   Split   Rather than divide
Commit   We are multiplied
To unconditional love
And then   Families
                                                                                        Gatherings
                                                                                        Celebrations
                                                                                        Friendships
                                                                                        Glee

E   x   p   a   n   d

Exponentially

Healing

I can't describe
The vastness
Of knowing
I haven't arrived
[I'll never arrive]

I am speechless at
The endless hope
Of constant
New horizons
[I'll forever strive]

The miles behind me
The miles ahead
The pain
Ohhhhhhhhhh
That ever-present dread

These shoes brought me to
Untold heights
Helped me scramble out of
Unfathomable lows
They've gotta lotta miles left

Every day
I lace them up again

I know it's about how I rise
And how far I'm willing to go

My left shoe is named
Persistence
My right
Resilience

Onward
Upward

Also
Just

Fuck

Dinner for Two

I sit to eat
A meal
Longed for all my life

With two life
Partners
Present
Living

I drink from
The Cup of Life
Eagerly tasting
Every word we speak

Thirstily imbibing
Infinite possibilities

Drunkenly dreaming
Of life with you

My cup
FULL

My life
O v e r
f
l
o
w
i
n
g

Saving Grace

I used to believe
With all of my heart and soul
That the rest of humanity
[Especially my family]
Would be set free
If
They were just like
Me

I believed this so
Earnestly
My way
ONE way

THE WAY

Then I had a child of my own
A child with a strength
I'd never known

My child forged me

I was truly
Set free

Like a hymn
I used to sing
"I once was blind
But now I see"

There are billions
Upon billions
Of beautiful ways
To be

None of them
Right
None of them
Wrong

All of them authentic
When worn by the strong

Baggage

You decided to leave
Tossing my sense of
Self-worth
Self-love
Security
In with your belongings

Away you went
My worth was spent

At the age of one
My Self
Was undone

A lifetime plagued
By a false impression

I had to retrieve
Me
From your possession

At age forty-nine
I reclaimed
Me
As
Mine

My Self you may have packed
But the singular thing I lacked
Was the paramount perception
Of my own inherent perfection

Your leaving
No longer impacts
My
Perceiving

I am intact

A Winter Blessing

When winter's as deep
As the night is long
And cold threatens
To freeze your song

May memories of spring delight your soul
Verdant hills with butterflies aflutter
Bulbs bursting into brilliant blooms
Bees buzzing and bathing in nectar

May the summer sun's
Warm and golden rays
Caress you gently
On your darkest days

May fall's kiss linger
A soft reminder
Colorful and crisp falling leaves
Symbolize needed surrender

May the sweetness of life meet you
In the bitterness of winter-long
Slowly warming your heart
Freeing your frozen song

My Dancing Place

My body
My playground
Sensations dance
With abandon

Diving from
The heights of
My mind
Into the depths of
My body

I feel
My feet
Keeping tempo
My hands
Floating skyward
My body
Finding rhythm
My hips
Swaying
My head
Tilting back
My eyes
Close
My body
O P E N S

I feel
Sensual
Beautiful
Powerful
Trust-full
Graceful
Faithful
FREE

I feel
Me

Descent

Night descends
And so do I
Into the deep end
Behind my eyes

Before the plunge
My limbs flail
I fill my lungs
To no avail

I feel it coming
I fall still
The pain so stunning
It can't be real

This understanding
Has no meaning
I find myself spinning
At each nightly feeding

I know I'm not sane
I can't stay here
Tricked by shame
Hobbled by fear

My eyes can't be trusted
Nor my ears
My limbs are busted
My cheeks wet with tears

Nothing left to do
I open wide for it all
I let it flow through
Without breaking its fall

It slips and it slides
With incredible ease
And I finally find
A safe harbor in me

Surrender

When leaves have served their
Purpose
Trees cling to them
No longer

Falling leaves signify
Self-preservation

When resources are scarce
She reclaims
The life-giving nutrients
Held sacred
Within Her leaf

Ancient wisdom allows Her this
Knowing

This leaf has contributed
All that it possibly could
In its current form

She lets go

She understands that a new
Purpose
Will be forged upon its soft
Landing

She will repeat this process
With each precious leaf
That has served Her well

Preparing beneath Her
A warm winter blanket

She will survive
And eventually
Thrive
Again

And again
And again
And again

This is
Her Purpose

Liberty

When I was a child
Discomfort was
Normal
Uncertainty
Rampant
Fear
Rabid

They were my
Constant
Companions

I faced a
Lamb
Who became a
Lion
With little
Warning

I never figured out his
Trigger

When he pulled it
My illusion of
Peace
Shattered once again
With an ear-piercing
Roar
Like cracking ice
On a winter's pond
That ~~couldn't~~
Wouldn't
Hold my
Weight

I
Was
Swallowed

Frozen

My closet
My refuge

The darkness
The door
They cloaked me in
Temporary safety

I don't remember much
I do remember
The night I created a hole
At the top of that closet
So that Superman
Could fly in
Scoop me up
Fly me in his
Big
Strong arms
To an impenetrable
Castle of ice

The Fortress of Solitude

A part of me has
Remained there
With him
Ever since

I return to her
Hold her in my safe
Embrace
Whispering
That she is free
To come back to
Me

That lion's
Roar
His sharpened
Claws
And open
Maw
Control us
No longer

She and Me
Claim our
Liberty
From
The lion
The closet
The fortress
The solitude

We step forward
Together
Onto the ice
That holds
Unwavering
Under our
Trusting
Feet

Destinations

I am moving toward
Grace and sacred space
In the form of
An infinity symbol

Reciprocal
Receiving
Releasing
Unconditional Love

A home
Not a house
Decorated with photographs
Dotted with smudged fingerprints
Left as reminders
Abundant life

An old
Comfortable cottage
Filled with family

A whole life to explore
Within those brightly painted
Cheerful walls

Two explorers
Resilient
Persistent
Find the key
A locked room opens wide
To wander
And wonder
O Yes!

A wild and random garden
Bursting with color
Food for the
Soul-body
Weeds welcome
Defenses forgotten

A husband
Gently caressing
Life
From all that he touches

Hand in hand
A father and daughter
Walking together
Compassionately tending
To our wounds
Securing a future of freedom
From shame
Grounded in empathy
My hand atop his
Sealing our connection
With a pat

Reciprocal
Receiving
Releasing
Unconditional Love

Free to be me

Safe
At last

Artist Statement

The poems I have penned all have one goal: transmutation. Creativity is the conduit that channels my emotions through the wastelands of my mind toward the fertile deltas of my body, heart, and soul, where they find release. Along this invisible conduit, my words become powerful feelings that call out to their roots, spread out like mycelium all along the path before them. Childhood traumas have found comfort and safety within my mind and body, seeping poison into those root systems, profoundly impacting my life and health.

When I look back on my life, it is as if I am looking at a mirror that fell from a wall, gazing upon shattered pieces of various shapes and sizes; some flung out of reach, some swept up and thrown away, others so damaged that I can't be sure of what I'm seeing. This shattering has had lifelong impacts on my relationships with myself, the men in my life, my child, and the faith I still manage to hold precious outside of organized religion. This is the very real impact of PTSD on me.

During my childhood, safety was my primary need. Dark, deep hiding spaces were invaluable, both physically and emotionally. My mother, sister, and I found safety, comfort, and joy in the new home and lives our mother carefully cultivated. I was fifteen, and it would take years to realize how much healing I needed. My first two marriages (the former lasting three years, the latter nearly eighteen) couldn't have been more different. The only similarity was that I showed up in them as my little girl self, starved for love and affection from a masculine presence, with a shattered concept of self. How others perceived me was how I perceived myself. I was spectacularly codependent without comprehending its poisonous impact. After my second marriage fell apart, I confronted myself for the very first time in my life. I began a healing journey that continues to this day.

When I started writing, I discovered that not only was I controlled, I was controlling myself. Not only was I abandoned, I had abandoned myself. Not only was I abused, I was abusing myself. My writing allowed me to dig deep enough to find that only through embracing myself in all of my imperfections, and bathing in my own unconditional Love, could I finally find empowerment as a divine feminine creation. I am whole and perfect, just as I am.

I now enjoy a life where I show up as myself, for myself, and for those I love (most of the time). Practicing this new way of being has allowed me to experience Love in a profoundly healing soulmate union, a sacred space I treasure. The most valuable gift I have received is that I now understand my worth and sacredness, apart from the messages I received from past and present patriarchal, paternal impositions.

Today, I am safe. I am supported. I am powerful. I am empowered. My poetry allows the dark and twisty sheltering passages of my youth to once again flood with light. Seeping sadness becomes weeping wisdom, and I find my way back to my soul.

I am FREE.

At least, I'm working on it.

Epilogue

I went into my darkness to find my light. Counterintuitive, yes. Yet that is exactly what happened. Curating and creating this anthology allowed me to curate and create a new me.

I have written poetry as an outlet for my emotional landscape since I was young, but I had never before felt the desire to publish it, nor to delve any deeper than each individual poem required of me. This work is not of me. Other than divine intervention, I have no other way of understanding it. I experienced myriad miracles throughout the process of this work coming through me, which is how I choose to view what some might call "luck," or "coincidence." I met folks who came into my life right on time to support me with various aspects of this project that I did not have the skill set to perform. Benefactors generously shared their time, unique talents, words of affirmation, and unbidden monetary support. I let go of many lifelong coping mechanisms that were no longer serving me as an adult, and which had become toxic physically, mentally, spiritually, and emotionally.

One of my personal goals in the writing of my chapter was to share it with those whom it was about—if I felt safe in doing so. When I felt that my chapter was ready to share, I invited my mother and sister to my dinner table for a reading. We laughed, we cried, and we deeply communed. I felt seen, heard, and held by them like never before. I shared my chapter with my former husband and his wife. I went to their beautiful home. I sat next to them at the dinner table that used to be our dinner table. I read every word to them. I shared emotions and experiences that I wish I had the words, the understanding, and the willingness to share during our nearly eighteen-year marriage. It was profound to go into the darkness together. It was even more magical to enter into the light together on the other side.

Then, twenty-five years after I last saw my birth father and the month that I was announcing the publication of our anthology, he reappeared. My earlier attempts to see him were driven by subconscious control, fear, or rage—probably all three—mixed into a toxic cocktail. I now understand, utterly, that I was being protected. It wasn't yet time. I had so much work to do before I could receive him in the way that I needed to receive him: with unconditional Love and compassion.

I tried to force a premature meeting with my birth father in the fall of 2021. I sent him a message saying that I wanted to see him. We set a date. When it came time for the meeting, he didn't show. I didn't hear from him until the following day. Even though he apologized, I felt re-abandoned. When I worked up the courage to email him a copy of my chapter as publication loomed, I didn't receive a response. I felt abandoned yet again. Five months before we finally reconnected, I was guided to find my ability to release the rage, fear, and control that I harbored, unknowingly, for most of my life.

When my cousin, Chandler, called in the spring of 2023, I was spiraling in the toxic soup of rage, fear, and control that I had been subconsciously simmering in for most of my life. With great sensitivity and empathy, he asked me if I needed to release anything before publication. He is an intuitive healer, a beautiful soul. I have trusted him all of my life. I shared my story about my birth father with him. He guided me to see that I had been nurturing rage, and he shared a story with me in return. A story of release.

I took Chan's experience and designed one of my own, intuitively. While lying on my back on my bed, I decided to invite The Creator to guide me toward release through meditation. I lit some incense, held some crystals that comforted me, prayed, and dove in. I immediately saw my toddler self on a bridge in a Japanese garden in San Francisco. This is a familiar "memory" for me, as my mother described my last visit with my birth father here many times. I was holding his hand, looking up at him with tears in my eyes. My whole being was willing him to stay with me. I knew my mother was waiting for me, but I needed more time, a lifetime more. As I stared into his eyes, I felt the need to verbally express out loud to him everything my little girl self, and my adult self, wanted him to know. Needed him to know. These words and feelings needed OUT.

"I look for you everywhere. I can't find you no matter how hard I look. I NEED YOU. Every man I've ever loved was an expression of my need for you. I was vulnerable when you left me! I AM ANGRY THAT YOU AREN'T HERE TO PROTECT ME…

Every time I see a daddy with his daughter, my heart breaks…

I miss you…

I love you…

I forgive you."

What started as whispers built to a screaming crescendo, followed by tearful acceptance. My ears dripped with my tears. The words that I screamed flowed from the rage I had nurtured over the fifty years since I had been abandoned. I didn't realize that it had been seeking an outlet for all those decades.

I was in awe of the transformation I felt inside of me, so I asked who I needed to talk to next. What followed, in succession, was a similar experience with each person I had been harboring rage for. My throat ached from the yelling, the crying, the flow of thick, hot, black rage that continued to burst from me like a geyser. The rage flowed until the source bled dry, as did my tears. Peace, forgiveness, unconditional Love, and even JOY began to bubble up in its place. I was surrounded by a nurturing light. It felt like a hug. I rested in it. When I finally opened my eyes, an hour had passed. I savored the bliss that enveloped me.

I let go of the control and fear that was driving me to contact my birth father. I allowed faith to take over, and I rested in the knowledge that what was happening was right on time and was happening for me rather than to me.

Five months later, on my birthday, he reached out to me through Facebook Messenger. I ugly-cried when I saw the notification. The tears flowed from a place of relief, gratitude, amazement, and HOPE. Four days later, I felt grounded enough to respond. This time, my response was filled with the vibration of Love. I asked to meet him. He immediately responded with the same loving vibration, and I knew intuitively that this time would be different.

We met that Sunday for brunch, which turned into afternoon coffee, which turned into hors d'oeuvres. We shared six precious hours of deep-diving, truth-telling, accountability offering, and compassionate conversation. He sat next to me in the coffee shop and read every word I wrote in my chapter, debriefing with me after each poem, delighting my soul with his easy understanding of my words. Of my heart. All I could do was sit in wonder. This was actually happening. It was surreal.

It is a beginning. Our hearts are open. We are open. This book forged a path between us. Gratitude precedes each step we take, together.

I am a new creation.

Afterword
By Kirsten Fountain

We begin this life as a seed, holding limitless potential. As our seed grows roots, seeking nourishment, we form what the rest of the world can witness above the ground: Our trunks and canopies serve to reach for, collect, and distribute energy from the sun. While underground, our roots provide our tree with a needed anchor and life-giving water and nutrients. As our trees adapt to the environment in which they are rooted, their forms change to survive.

When we came together at the beginning of this project, we knew we needed nourishment, support, and community. With these needs met, we had faith that our forms could completely change as we found new ways to reach for the sun.

Our co-creators eagerly took hold of our shovels and picks, digging into the fertile soil that houses our root wounds. We have each journeyed deeply, some finding more than anticipated, others knowing precisely what we buried. As we faced what we unearthed, we discovered new paths to nourishment, with support. We are courageous, yes. And we also understand that we are all safe—right here, right now, where we are digging. While this fact did not protect us from the uprooted feelings, patterns, defensive parts, traumas, and root wounds that still impact us today, we understand that feelings are transitory. Our feelings, patterns, defensive parts, traumas, and root wounds, just like our brains, are plastic. We can work with them: rewiring, breaking, and bandaging them in the present, where we can redirect them. As a result, our possibilities are ever brighter, more expansive, and more hopeful than we imagined before picking up those shovels and picks.

We are still healing; many of us have the support of trauma-informed therapists or tools that we learned through therapy as we do this work for ourselves and for those we love.

Now that we have perspective: we are no longer afraid, controlled, or stuck in past versions of ourselves. Those feelings may come to visit, creating temporary storms, but they no longer dictate our lives because we can see ourselves from the top of the mighty tree that we are becoming. We now see that our roots and branches are still growing—seeking and finding what will nourish us as we continue reaching higher and ever higher.

The highest-reaching trees in the world are the majestic redwoods, which grow in communities. When storms rage through a grove of redwoods, they are rarely toppled because their root systems intentionally intertwine, allowing them to be supported as they sway with the inevitable cycles of nature.

We know that our possibilities are endless as we form and re-form, rooted firmly in the support and nourishment we receive from our community. Like a grove of redwoods, we are stronger when we are held through life's storms. We are better together.

If you would like more insight into our process or are interested in how you can begin this work for yourself, please visit freeingourfrozensongs.com to access our workbook, tools, and meditations.

* 9 7 8 1 9 6 2 9 9 6 1 3 6 *